Ein Kurzkurs für Erwachsene

ACTIVATE
YOUR ENGLISH

Intermediate Self-study Workbook

**mit Glossar
englisch-deutsch**

**Barbara Sinclair
Philip Prowse**

D1728971

CAMBRIDGE
UNIVERSITY PRESS

Ernst Klett Verlag
Stuttgart München Düsseldorf Leipzig

PUBLISHED BY THE PRESS SYNDICATE OF THE UNIVERSITY OF CAMBRIDGE
The Pitt Building, Trumpington Street, Cambridge CB2 1RP, United Kingdom

CAMBRIDGE UNIVERSITY PRESS
The Edinburgh Building, Cambridge CB2 1RU, United Kingdom
40 West 20th Street, New York, NY10011-4211, USA
10 Stamford Road, Oakleigh, Melbourne 3166, Australia

First published 1996

Weitere Bestandteile von *Activate Your English Intermediate:*

Coursebook (deutsche Ausgabe)	Klett-Nr. 3-12-531121-7
Teacher's Book	Klett-Nr. 3-12-531123-3
Class Cassette	Klett-Nr. 3-12-531124-1
Self-study Workbook Cassette	Klett-Nr. 3-12-531125-X
Self-study Workbook CD	Klett-Nr. 3-12-531126-8

1. Auflage   1 3 2 1 | 1999 98 97

Alle Drucke dieser Auflage können im Unterricht
nebeneinander benutzt werden, sie sind untereinander
unverändert.
Die letzte Zahl bezeichnet das Jahr dieses Druckes.

© Cambridge University Press 1996
© für diese Ausgabe:
Ernst Klett Verlag GmbH, Stuttgart 1997.
Alle Rechte vorbehalten.

Druck: University Press, Cambridge.
Printed in Great Britain.

ISBN 3-12-531122-5

INHALT

VORWORT

Das *Activate Your English Intermediate Self-study Workbook* enthält 16 Units für das Selbststudium. In den Übungen werden Wortschatz und Fertigkeiten aus den *Coursebook* Units wiederholt; so stehen Ihnen zusätzlich 15 bis 20 Stunden für die vertiefende Arbeit zu Hause zur Verfügung. Für jede *Self-study Workbook* Unit benötigt man etwa 45 bis 60 Minuten.

Die Units beinhalten Grammatik- und Wortschatzübungen, Lese- und Hörverstehensübungen sowie nützliche Lerntips. Außerdem gibt es vier „Listening Practice" Units, in denen Sie Ihr Hörverständnis verbessern sowie den Wortschatz und die Grammatik aus dem *Coursebook* vertiefen können.

Die zu diesem Buch gehörige *Self-study Workbook Cassette / CD* können Sie ebenfalls im Selbststudium verwenden. Sie enthält Hörverstehens-, Aussprache- und Intonationsübungen.

Bei regelmäßiger Durchführung der Übungen im *Self-study Workbook* werden Sie größere Fortschritte machen und mehr von der Fremdsprache behalten. Es empfiehlt sich, nach Beendigung einer *Coursebook* Unit die dazugehörige *Self-study Workbook* Unit zu Hause durchzuarbeiten.

Im Anhang des Buches finden Sie Lösungsschlüssel, Hörtexte und ein umfassendes englisch-deutsches Glossar.

Ich wünsche Ihnen viel Freude und Erfolg mit *Activate Your English*.

Barbara Sinclair

Philip Prowse

Barbara Sinclair   Philip Prowse

1

Grammar: the gerund

In this extract from a guide to Madagascar the author gives advice to tourists who want to visit remote country villages.

a) Read the extract and choose the correct form of the verbs in brackets.

Some cultural dos and don'ts

Remember (1 to follow/following) the rules that govern society in Madagascar. Human relationships depend on two basic standards of behaviour: (2 to show/showing) respect for the other person and (3 to know/knowing) one's place in society.

Visitors to a village take the first step by (4 introduce/introducing) themselves to the *Ray aman-dreny* (the village elders and rulers). When shaking hands the visitors put their hand out first. Villagers may not be used to (5 meet/meeting) *vahaza*, as foreigners are called, so it is important (6 to be/being) polite.

At a village party or meeting it is customary (7 to pass/passing) around a common bowl of liquid from which everyone drinks. Visitors should accept this drink which may be coffee, water or rum (*betsabetsa*). Sit on the ground like everyone else, especially if a mat is provided for the purpose.

There is no point in (8 to stand/standing) when everyone else is seated.

When leaving a village always say goodbye (*Tsofy rano izahay*) to the elders. Ask permission before walking across a rice field.

The Malagasy enjoy (9 to make/making) speeches. When giving a speech it is usual to apologise for your inadequacy. Do not interrupt an elder when he is speaking.

A man walks in front of a woman, and goes in front of her up and down stairs.

Do not touch or caress babies, or touch a baby's head.

Do not pay a man a compliment on his wife's or daughter's clothes.

Do not sit on the bed of an elder or young girl.

Avoid (10 step/stepping) over a straw mat, particularly one on which people eat.

Adapted from *Guide to Madagascar* edited by Hilary Bradt

b) Complete these sentences about Madagascar.

1 You must avoid _____ on a young girl's bed.

2 You must allow an elder to finish _____ a speech.

3 The Malagasy are used to _____ on the ground.

4 The Malagasy enjoy _____ from a common bowl at parties.

5 It's a good idea to practise _____ the Malagasy language.

2

Vocabulary: occupations and places of work

Match the occupations, the activities and the places.

Example

Occupation	Activity	Place
Teacher	I teach geography	Secondary school

Occupation	Activity	Place
1 Actor	I repair cars	Secondary school
2 Waiter	I play the violin	University
3 Teacher	I run a shop	Hospital
4 Burglar	I look after your teeth	Surgery
5 Business executive	I bring your food	Theatre
	I study theory	Shop
6 Steward	I work for the government	Office
7 Civil servant		The army
8 Computer operator	I break in and steal	Airline
	I serve food on planes	Restaurant
9 Soldier	I write newspapers	Your house
10 Dentist	I welcome you on arrival	Hotel
11 Engineer		Garage
12 Shop assistant	I care for sick people	Orchestra
13 Journalist	I make money	
14 Manager	I can use a gun	
15 Mechanic	I input data	
16 Musician	I teach geography	
17 Nurse	I design bridges	
18 Professor	I type letters and answer the phone	
19 Receptionist	I perform in plays	
20 Secretary	I work in a shop	

3

Intonation

Listen to these questions from Exercise 4 (a) of the Coursebook. Mark each question to show if it ends with the voice rising ↗ or falling ↘. Listen again and repeat the questions.

1 Is it time for lunch?

2 Do you have any children?

3 The plane's quite full, isn't it?

4 What's your name?

5 Do you know when lunch is?

6 How much do you earn?

7 Can I borrow your newspaper, please?

8 What do you do?

9 Are you married?

10 Are you going to Rio?

11 Do you know what the time is, please?

12 How old are you?

13 How much did your jacket cost?

14 Is there anything in the newspaper?

15 Who do you vote for?

4

Classroom English

Get the best out of your teacher! Put the jumbled words in the right order to make sentences you can use when you want help from your teacher.

1 me excuse mean what word this does ?

_____

2 please again say that you can ?

_____

3 don't afraid quite I understand I'm.

_____

4 that do spell please you how ?

_____

5 'I like' say not you 'I'm liking' and why do ?

_____

6 pronounce please how you this do word ?

_____

7 correct excuse this is me ?

_____

8 'engineer' spell this is how you ?

_____

Listen to the cassette and check your answers.

5

Your test

Choose a paragraph from Unit 1 of the Coursebook (e.g. from 'How to be a Carioca') or from another English book. Record your text on a cassette or ask another person to read it to you. The text should be read once quickly, then once slowly, and then once quickly again.

Listen to your cassette or the reader and write the text. Then compare it with the original.

Learning tip

Setting yourself a test once like this is useful. But you will get much more benefit if you get into the habit of testing yourself regularly. Save your tests and do them again after a month or two. You'll be surprised at how much easier they are then.

1
Grammar: 'like/would like'

Complete the text with 'like' plus gerund or 'would like' plus infinitive.

Example

I *like discussing* (discuss) language learning and never miss an opportunity. One day I *would like to write* (write) a book about it,' the new teacher said. 'I already have,' the other teacher replied.

Interview with a teacher

A problem that some students have is that although they _____ (1 speak) English in class, they are afraid to do so outside class. 'I _____ (2 talk) to foreign visitors in English,' a student told me, 'but I'm always afraid of making mistakes.' Another problem is that some students _____ (3 learn) English without doing any work! They've read these advertisements saying 'Learn a language in 36 hours!' and believe them. Now few people _____ (4 learn) vocabulary or spelling rules for hours at a time but some hard work is necessary. I _____ (5 see) smaller class sizes and more hours a week for English, but I don't expect it will happen. In fact I quite _____ (6 teach) large classes, but it is difficult to give students individual attention. What I really _____ (7 do) is take my students to England for a few weeks but so far I have been put off by the cost.

2
Grammar: defining

Match the people/things and their definitions.

A microchip	is someone who	makes people laugh.
A comedian	is something which	heats food.
A teenager		has retired.
A microwave		cares about the environment.
A pensioner		has been to university.
A candidate		rejects society.
A 'green'		controls a computer.
A graduate		is between 13 and 19.
A drop-out		is applying for a job.

Examples

A thinker is someone who wants to know why.
A vacuum cleaner is something which sucks up dirt.

Look back at Exercise 2 in Self-study Workbook Unit 1 and make up sentences about the occupations there.

Example

An actor is someone who performs in plays.

3
Pronunciation: silent letters

Listen to the cassette and repeat the words.

Listen again and underline the letters which are not pronounced when the words are said at normal speed.

Example

int<u>e</u>resting

interested	secretary
business	several
literature	average
comfortable	medicine
different	favourite
listening	vegetable
vocabulary	

4
Classroom English: grammar words

Study the short list of grammar terms and look at the examples.

Grammar term	Examples
verb	go, look
noun	job, word
infinitive	to study, to look
gerund	studying, working
conjunction	and, but, when, so
adjective	short
definite article	the
indefinite article	a, an
subject pronoun	I, you, he, she, it, we, they
object pronoun	me, you, him, her, it, us, them
possessive pronoun	mine, yours, his, hers, its, ours, theirs
reflexive pronoun	myself, yourself, himself, herself, itself, ourselves, yourselves, themselves
possessive adjective	my, your, his, her, its, our, your, their
preposition	of, at
adverb	quickly

Copy sentences from this unit or from a book and label as many grammar words as you can.

Example

definite
article   noun   verb gerund preposition noun
   ↓   ↓   ↓   ↓   ↓   ↓

    The Feeler enjoys being with people
    and learns through co-operation.
  ↗   ↑   ↑   ↑

conjunction verb preposition   noun

5
Your test

Choose five topic areas (e.g. holidays, houses, colours, animals, food). Make a list of 20 words in each area. Write the lists in a vertical line so that each word starts just below the previous one.

Then put a clean piece of paper over the list so that only the first letter shows. Complete the words on the piece of paper.

1

Grammar: present simple and past simple tenses

David Hockney is a famous English artist. Here are the first two paragraphs of his autobiography. Complete the paragraphs with the verbs in the list. You may use some verbs more than once.

I was born in Bradford in 1937. I (1) _____ three brothers and a sister. I (2) _____ the fourth child; I (3) _____ one younger brother. Two of them (4) _____ in Australia, my eldest brother still (5) _____ in Bradford, and my sister (6) _____ a district nurse in Bedfordshire. Until I (7) _____ eleven I (8) _____ to the local council school in Bradford, where my brothers and sister (9) _____ . Then I (10) _____ to Bradford Grammar School on a scholarship; my eldest brother had also had a scholarship there but he (11) _____ the school the year I (12) _____ in 1948. My other brothers (13) _____ to a different school. I always (14) _____ I (15) _____ it. I (16) _____ not really happy there; I (17) _____ probably too bored.

At the age of eleven I (18) _____ in my mind that I (19) _____ to be an artist, but the meaning of the word 'artist' to me then (20) _____ very vague – the man who (21) _____ Christmas cards (22) _____ an artist, the man who (23) _____ posters (24) _____ an artist, the man who just (25) _____ lettering for posters (26) _____ an artist. Anyone (27) _____ an artist who in his job (28) _____ to pick up and a brush and paint something.

From David Hockney by David Hockney

commenced	hated	live	wanted
decided	have	lives	was
did	is	painted	went
had	left	say	

2

Grammar: 'used to'

a) Think about yourself when you were younger. How have you changed? Write five sentences about yourself using 'used to'.

Examples

I used to wear short trousers.
I used to go to the beach every afternoon.
I used to have a model railway.

b) Write five more sentences about your family.

Examples

We used to have supper at six o'clock.
We used to live with my grandmother.
My father used to have a motorbike.

3

Grammar: present perfect tense

a) Write five sentences about your dreams, wishes, hopes and fears. Use 'never/always' and the present perfect tense.

Examples

I've always wanted a mountain bike.
I've never wanted to go to America.
I've always been afraid of the dark.

b) Write five questions about people's secret dreams. Use 'wanted to' + infinitive, 'thought of' + '-ing' and 'dreamed of' + '-ing'.

Examples

Have you ever thought of leaving home?
Have you ever dreamed of being rich?
Have you ever wanted to fly around the world?

Answer the questions for yourself.

4
Grammar: irregular verbs

Regular verbs form the past simple and the past participle with '-ed'. Irregular verbs form the past simple and past participle in different ways. There are three main types of irregular verb:

Type A

The infinitive, the past simple and the past participle are the same.

Example

hurt   hurt   hurt

Type B

The past simple and the past participle are the same.

Example

send   sent   sent

Type C

All three are different.

Example

speak   spoke   spoken

Decide if the following verbs are Type A, Type B or Type C, and write out the three parts of each verb as in the examples above.

1 cost cut hit let put shut set

2 get lose

3 sell tell

4 build spend

5 bleed feed hold lead read

6 become come run

7 hear make pay say

8 dream feel keep leave mean meet sleep

9 hang win

10 begin drink ring sing sink swim

11 bite hide

12 bring buy fight think catch teach

13 break choose steal

14 know grow throw

15 shake take

16 drive ride rise write

17 eat fall do fly forget give go see

5
Pronunciation: '-ed'

The ending '-ed' of regular verbs in the past is pronounced in three different ways:

Type A /ɪd/: wanted   decided

Type B /d/: opened   played

Type C /t/: looked   helped

Listen to the cassette and write 'A', 'B', or 'C' by each verb to show which group it belongs to. Then listen again and repeat the verbs.

1 accept	14 describe	27 invite	40 recommend
2 agree	15 disappear	28 join	41 refuse
3 ask	16 discuss	29 knock	42 request
4 answer	17 dress	30 listen	43 retire
5 attach	18 expect	31 miss	44 show
6 bath	19 explain	32 need	45 start
7 believe	20 finish	33 note	46 sunbathe
8 call	21 follow	34 notice	47 talk
9 check	22 gather	35 open	48 test
10 compare	23 greet	36 perform	49 tip
11 cook	24 happen	37 pick	50 travel
12 correct	25 help	38 prepare	51 wash
13 decline	26 interview	39 reach	52 wonder

6
Classroom English: punctuation

.   ,   ;   :   —

!   ?   " "   (   )

-    +   =   *

Listen to the cassette and write down what you hear.

1 _____   9 _____

2 _____   10 _____

3 _____   11 _____

4 _____   12 _____

5 _____   13 _____

6 _____   14 _____

7 _____   15 _____

8 _____

7
Your test

Take a passage from one of the reading or listening texts in this book or from some other book. Copy out the passage, leaving gaps where the verbs are. Write the verbs in a list at the bottom of the passage. Put the passage away. The next day take the passage out and write the verbs in the correct place.

1

Grammar: 'will' and 'going to' future

Complete this passage using 'will' or 'going to'.

Martin is not so sure about the future. But he (1) _____ know more when he gets his examination results in ten days' time. He (2) _____ (not) wait for a letter with the results. Instead he (3) _____ go into school the day the results arrive. The rest of the summer is more or less planned: he (4) _____ go on holiday to Malta after the examination results and then he expects to find work in a factory. He hopes that the factory (5) _____ need him because he needs the money. His plans for the autumn are clear. 'After working in the factory I (6) _____ go to Italy. I (7) _____ spend three months in Perugia learning Italian. I know that learning Italian (8) _____ be quite hard but hopefully I (9) _____ succeed. After Italy, I don't know. I want to go to Africa but I don't know if I (10) _____ have enough money.'

2

Reading: Nelson Mandela, 1956

At his trial in 1956 Nelson Mandela made a speech about the future. Complete the text with these infinitives:

to be	to do	to live	to seek
to be paid	to have	to own	to travel

You may need to use an infinitive more than once.

Africans want (1) _____ a living wage. Africans want (2) _____ work which they are capable of doing, and not work which the government says they are capable of. Africans want (3) _____ where they obtain work, and not to be chased out of the area because they were not born there. Africans want (4) _____ land in places where they work, and not be obliged (5) _____ in rented houses which they can never call their own. We want (6) _____ part of the general population, and not confined to living in ghettos. African men want (7) _____ their wives and children to live with them where they work, and not be forced into an unnatural existence in men's hostels. African women want (8) _____ with their menfolk and not be left permanently widowed in the reserves. We want (9) _____ in our own country and (10) _____ work where we want to and not where the Labour Bureau tells us to. We want a just share in the whole of South Africa; we want security and a stake in society.

From *Nelson Mandela* by Mary Benson

3

Pronunciation: the alphabet

a) Put the letters of the alphabet into groups which have the same sound when we spell words aloud.

Examples

A has the same sound as K and H.
L has the same sound as M.
P has the same sound as T.
I has the same sound as Y.

Listen to the cassette and check your answers.

b) Look at the cartoon. It is about two men at a pub in England, where you have to be 18 years old to have an alcoholic drink. The dialogue in the cartoon uses the sounds of the letters. The first bit of conversation goes:

L.O.! = Hello!

2 G.n.T. = Two G and T (gin and tonics).

A? = Eh?

Look through the cartoon and try to work out the dialogue.

Listen to the cassette and check your answers.

Adapted from a cartoon by Posy Simmonds

4

Classroom English: instructions and questions

Listen to the cassette and decide if the teacher is asking a question (Q) or giving an instruction (I).

Examples

[I] Could you please work in pairs?

[Q] Has anyone got a dictionary?

1 ☐   5 ☐   8 ☐

2 ☐   6 ☐   9 ☐

3 ☐   7 ☐   10 ☐

4 ☐

5

Your test

Look back through the written work you have done so far and find spelling mistakes you have made. Make a list of the words you spelt wrongly. Then look up the words in a dictionary and write a list of the definitions of the words (as you used them, not all the meanings). Don't write the words themselves. So now you have a list of definitions. Put the list away for a day or two. Then write the words which are defined by the definitions and check that they are spelt correctly.

Example

Definition	Word
used for cutting	knife

LISTENING PRACTICE 1

1

Using Listening Practice units

This is the first of four special Listening Practice units in your Self-study Workbook (you will find the others after Unit 8, after Unit 12 and after Unit 16). These Listening Practice units will give you the opportunity to practise listening to natural spoken English. There are activities for you to carry out and answers and tapescripts at the back of this book so that you can check how well you understand the recordings.

Learning tips

1 If you want to improve your listening, don't look at the tapescript before you listen. In real life you rarely read something before you hear it.

2 Use the tapescript when you have finished listening or if you have a problem.

3 Afterwards, make use of the recording or the tapescript for learning or practising language you are interested in (see next column for suggestions).

Suggested activities

When you have completed the listening activities in the book, you can use the recordings in other ways, too, according to your own needs and preferences. You might want to focus on vocabulary, specific grammar points, speaking fluently, etc. Here are some examples of what you could do:

a) Listen again and write a summary of the main points. Then check the tapescript for the content.

b) Look at the tapescript and make a note of any new words or phrases you want to learn.

c) Look at the tapescript and underline specific grammatical structures you want to focus on.

d) Make a photocopy of the tapescript and blank out every fifth or sixth word with corrector fluid. Then listen to the recording and fill in the gaps.

e) Listen to the recording, but stop it after every sentence and repeat it aloud.

f) Play the recording and stop it now and again in the middle of a sentence. Guess how the sentence ends and then play the recording to see if you were right.

g) Listen to the recording and read the tapescript aloud at the same time, at the same speed.

h) Record yourself reading the tapescript aloud (perhaps with friends) and compare it with the original.

i) Listen to the recording and write down what you hear. Then compare your version with the tapescript.

You will find other ideas to use by looking at the units in the Coursebook.

2

Darling brother

Daniella is talking about her brother. Listen to her and decide which of the summaries on the next page is accurate.

a) Daniella hated her brother, who was three years younger than her, and she tried to kill him three times on purpose. First, when he was a baby in his pram, she tried to suffocate him with cushions. Then, when he was about two, she tried to poison him with orange-flavoured children's aspirin which she made into 'soup' on her doll's cooker. Their mother was hysterical. Finally, when they were much older she tried to strangle him in a fight. However, she didn't succeed.

b) Daniella tried to kill her brother, who was three years younger than her, three times. However, only one of these attempts was on purpose. First, when he was a baby, she picked him up and threw him out of his pram because he looked cold. Later on, when he was two, she gave him some aspirin 'soup' made on her doll's cooker and he became unconscious. Finally, when they were much older, they had a nasty fight, and she really wanted to kill him. Luckily, her brother is still alive.

c) Daniella almost killed her brother, who was three years younger than her, three times. However, the first two times weren't on purpose. Firstly, when he was a baby, she covered up his face with cushions because she thought he looked cold. Secondly, when she was a bit older, she made him some 'soup' from orange-flavoured children's aspirin on her doll's cooker, and he became unconscious. Lastly, they had a nasty fight when they were older, and she really wanted to kill him, but she didn't succeed.

d) Daniella tried to kill her brother, who was three years older than her, several times because she hated him. First, when she was three, she tried to cover his face with cushions when he was in his pram so he couldn't breathe. When she was about ten, she tried to poison him with aspirin 'soup' made on her doll's cooker. Then, she poured salt water into his mouth to make him sick. Finally, when they were much older, he nearly killed her in a fight, but he didn't succeed.

5 Family life

1

Grammar: simple and first conditional

a) Simple conditional

Join the two halves of the sentences below.

Example
If I catch a cold, I take lots of vitamins.

1	If I catch a cold,	a)	if you use e-mail.
2	People can only help	b)	I take lots of vitamins.
3	If I watch too much TV,	c)	if you take regular exercise.
4	If you want to pass your exams,	d)	if they know what's going on.
5	You feel much better	e)	I get a headache.
6	You save time	f)	you have to revise frequently.

b) First conditional

Join the two halves of the sentences below.

Example
If Treasure has her own phone, she won't do any homework.

1	If Treasure has her own phone,	a)	if you do the shopping.
2	If someone rings late at night,	b)	you'll lose weight.
3	If you review your learning regularly,	c)	if they split up.
4	If you switch to low-fat foods,	d)	Treasure won't sleep.
5	You'll reduce stress and tension	e)	she won't do any homework.
6	I'll clean the kitchen	f)	if they keep on arguing.
7	Their marriage will break up	g)	if you take up meditation.
8	The children will suffer	h)	you'll make more progress.

2

Learner training: appropriacy

We speak to our friends in a different way from the way we speak to strangers. The way we write a personal letter is different from the way we write a business letter. We choose our vocabulary and expressions according to our audience.

Read this magazine article and try to find words or expressions which are out of place. For example, look at the first sentence which ends 'mum, dad and two kids'. This is how we might talk to a friend but is not what we expect in an article, where 'mother, father and two children' is more appropriate. Replace other inappropriate expressions with expressions from the list.

man	people	for example	grandmother and grandfather
is not uncommon	limits	Such extended families	
are much more common	children	is scarce	wife
			It is most common

Families around the world

The common image of the family in the West is the nuclear family: mum, dad and two kids. This image is no longer true of many Western societies where couples living together with no kids are the largest group, and where families frequently break up. The average size of a family in 1900 was 4.6; now it is 2.51. In Britain, just to take one case, one in five families have only one parent, and the global figure is between a quarter and a third of all families.

You get a lot more extended families in other parts of the world. In extended families two or more generations – parents, gran and grandpa, and children – live together, sometimes with more distant relatives. Great big families like this provide a support network that helps the kids and old folks to be looked after. You get it a lot in countries where a large family is vital as a source of labour.

The environment often influences the family. Polygamy, where a bloke has more than one missus, is often found where there is plenty of land and women produce much of the food, for example in southern Africa. Where there isn't much good land, polyandry, where a woman has more than one husband, happens quite a lot. The Nyinba people of Nepal in the Himalayas practise fraternal polyandry, where the husbands are brothers. This cuts down family size and means that several men can support one family.

Adapted from 'Families: is there a fitting image?' by Jane Watterson

3
Vocabulary: sounds

a) We make lots of noises with our mouth and nose. Listen to the cassette and choose the correct word to complete these sentences.

snore   sigh   sneeze   hiccup   yawn   pant   cough

Treasure wasn't feeling at all well. She had a really bad cold. 'I think I'm going to (1) _____,' she said. 'Aaatishoo!' Her throat was sore and she started to (2) _____ . She felt thirsty and drank a glass of cold water quickly, but this made her (3) _____ . She did some exercises but she was short of breath and started to (4) _____ . 'Oh, dear,' she said with a (5) _____ . She felt sleepy and this made her (6) _____ . Soon she was fast asleep on her back with her mouth open. She began to (7) _____ .

b) Dogs bark, lions roar and frogs croak. How about these animals and birds? Listen to the cassette and match the name, picture and sound.

Animal/bird		Sound	
cat	horse	bleat	mew
cow	sheep	hiss	moo
duck	snake	neigh	quack

4
Pronunciation

Listen to the sound at the end of these words:

father   mother   daughter   teacher

This sound is spelt in lots of different ways. Underline the letter or letters in these words which are pronounced with this sound.

amusing	approach	supposed	correct
apparently	away	banana	magazine
entertaining	finally	yoghurt	

Listen to the cassette, repeat and check your answers.

5
Classroom English: checking you understand

If you don't understand an explanation or an instruction in class, it's good to let the teacher know. Match the beginnings and endings of these sentences.

1 I'm afraid I'm not
2 Do you mean that you want us to
3 I'm sorry but we're not entirely sure
4 Could you please go over
5 What you mean is that we've
6 Am I right in thinking that
7 What page did you
8 I don't understand why it's
9 Excuse me, but are we meant
10 What do you want us to do after

a) we've finished?
b) want us to look at?
c) got to work in pairs.
d) quite sure what to do.
e) read the whole text?
f) to do it on our own?
g) what to do.
h) it again?
i) wrong.
j) 'treasure' means something valuable?

Listen to the cassette and check your answers.

6
Your test

Make up your own recorded oral test. First make a list of questions about families. Ask questions about people's ages, names, jobs and interests.

Examples
How many brothers and sisters do you have?
How old are they?
What are they called?
What do they do?
Are your grandparents still alive?
How old are they?
Where do they live?

Record your questions on a cassette, leaving spaces for the replies. Then play the cassette and interview yourself. If you press 'Record' after each question, you'll be able to record your answers.

6 My profile

1

Reading and listening

a) Read and listen to this poem by Brian Patten. Then look back to Exercise 3 in Unit 6 of the Coursebook. Is Helen a traveller in outer or inner space?

THE ASTRONAUT

We will take a trip
to the planets inside us,
where love is the astronaut

alone at last, not caring
what planet he lands on, and he,
free to glide between

what is said and
what is understood
by saying it,

sees how the Universe decays
while men find ways
of mending it.

From *Little Johnny's Confessions* by Brian Patten

b) Read this poem by Brian Patten and try to fill in the missing words.

Listen to the cassette and check your answers.

HAIR TODAY, NO HER TOMORROW

"I've been upstairs," she said.
"Oh yes?" I said.
"I found a hair," she said.
"A hair?" I said.
"In the bed," she said.
"From a head?" I said.
"It's not (1) _____," she said.
"Was it black?" I said.
"It was," she said.
"I'll (2) _____," I said.
"You swine," she said.
"Not quite," I said.
"I'm leaving," she said.
"Please don't," I said.
"I hate you!" she said.
"You do?" I said.
"Of (3) _____," she said.
"But (4) _____?" I said.
"That black hair," she said.
"A pity," I said.

"Time for truth," she said.
"For confessions?" I said.
"Me too," she said.
"You what?" I said.

"Someone else," she said.
"Oh (5) _____," I said.
"So there!" she said.
"Ah well," I said.
"Guess who?" she said.
"Don't (6) _____," I said.
"I will," she said.
"You would," I said.
"Your friend," she said.
"Oh damn," I said.
"And his (7) _____," she said.
"Him too?" I said.
"And the rest," she said.
"Good God," I said.

"What's that?" she said.
"What's (8) _____?" I said.
"That noise?" she said.
"Upstairs?" I said.
"Yes," she said.
"The new cat," I said.
"A (9) _____?" she said.
"It's black," I said.
"(10) _____?" she said.
"Long-haired," I said.

"Oh no," she said.
"Oh (11) _____," I said.
"Oh shit!" she said.
"Goodbye," I said.

"I lied," she said.
"You (12) _____?" I said.
"Of course," she said.
"About my (13) _____?" I said.
"Y-ess," she said.
"And the others?" I said.
"Ugh," she said.
"How odd," I said.
"I'm forgiven?" she said.
"Of course," I said.
"I'll stay?" she said.
"Please don't," I said.
"But why?" she said.
"I lied," I said.
"About what?" she said.
"The new cat," I said.
"It's (14) _____," I said.

From *Storm Damage* by Brian Patten

2
Vocabulary: compound adjectives

a) In the text in the Coursebook, Helen says that astronauts need to be hard-working. A person who works hard is a *hard-working* person. Use similar compound adjectives in these phrases.

1 a car which is moving slowly

2 a person who thinks quickly

3 someone who looks angry

4 someone who goes easily (takes things as they come)

5 someone who loves fun

b) We can also make compound adjectives like this: someone who has an open mind is an *open-minded* person. Use similar compound adjectives in these phrases.

1 someone who has a hard heart

2 someone who has a quick temper

3 someone who has brown eyes

4 someone with bad manners

5 someone with long hair

3
Vocabulary: adjective suffixes '-less' and '-ful'

The suffix '-ful' means 'full of' or 'having'. The suffix '-less' means 'without'.

Examples

thoughtful   full of thought
careless   without care

Which of the words below can take both suffixes and which can take only one?

care   power
doubt   price
harm   skill
hope   speech
pain   thought
peace   youth

4
Pronunciation

 Often not all the letters of a word are pronounced. For example, in 'flight' the 'gh' is silent. Listen to the cassette and underline the letters in these words which are not pronounced.

scientist   thumb
chocolate   thoughtful
written   straightforward
every   climb
people   hour
naturally   two
fascinated   know
mystery   answer
family   secretary
friends   half
fighter   talk

5
Classroom English: asking for help

Being able to ask your teacher or another student for help is very important. Put the words in these jumbled sentences into the right order.

1 understand I don't am I afraid

2 it please you over again could go ?

3 quite afraid I catch I'm you what said didn't

4 me excuse do how pronounce you word this ?

5 text difficulty I'm with having this

6 wrong this please you can why is explain ?

7 wrong understand I've don't done I what

8 this like pronounced word this is why ?

9 but sorry I I'm follow don't

10 what do to me excuse I know don't

🎞 Listen to the cassette to see if you were right.

6
Your test

Take a paragraph from the text in Unit 6 of the Coursebook or from a book. Write out each sentence separately with the words jumbled up, as in Exercise 5 above. Put the jumbled sentences away for a day or two. Then take them out and put the words back into the right order.

7 Some good advice

1

Grammar: second conditional

First, unscramble the words in column B to form sentences which give advice. (Remember to put in capital letters and punctuation.) Then match each piece of advice to a problem in column A.

A: Problems

1 I have problems understanding spoken English.

2 He still makes mistakes in the past tenses.

3 Her home is too noisy to study English.

4 My children aren't interested in learning English.

5 I'm terrible at spelling English words.

B: Advice

library if her I go to study would I the were to

_____

him I would if grammar get a were I book good

_____

television get I'd if you were a I

_____

you were if I write new down vocabulary times ten I would

_____

them video some buy cartoons I if I would were in you English

_____

2

Classroom English: negotiating and making suggestions

There are times when your teacher may ask you what you want to do next or when you would like to offer a suggestion to your teacher. The following expressions are useful because they are polite and not aggressive. Read and practise saying these expressions.

Perhaps it would be a good idea to . . .

I was wondering whether we could . . .

How about doing more listening activities like this one?

What about repeating this activity next time, to give us more practice?

I found this activity very useful. Could we do more like this, please?

I'm not sure this was very useful. Perhaps we could do something different next time?

3

Reading comprehension: Helpline

Helpline experts give you advice on your problems.

On the next page, match each letter with the correct piece of advice and draw an arrow (→) to connect them. (There are seven replies from Helpline, but only five problem letters here.)

1

Dear Helpline,

A few months ago when my boyfriend was away at a conference I met someone that I've always liked at a party. I behaved very badly. Several of my boyfriend's friends saw us. I told my boyfriend about it when he got back and apologised, but he's very cold to me now and goes on at me about my disloyalty. I regret it very much, but he won't forgive me.

a) Why don't you put up a large sign in your office saying what happened? If someone has accidentally taken your things, they will return them. It is a terrible thing when you can't trust the people you work with. If it happens again, you should report it to the security officer. If I were you, I would never leave my things where others can see them. Put your bag in a drawer and keep it locked.

2

Dear Helpline,

My parents divorced when I was 12 and I lost contact with my father. My aunt, his sister, later told me that my mother hated my father so much she stopped him seeing me. Now I've moved away from home I want to contact my father again. He's remarried and has another family. I'd love to get to know them, but I'm terrified they don't want to see me.

b) Why don't you explain the problem clearly to your boss? How about asking for a meeting with her? Tell her how long it takes to write a good report and ask that she gives you enough time in future. Tell her you can't work evenings any more (you could think of a good reason why not). Use the meeting to work out an action plan together.

3

Dear Helpline,

One of my friends only contacts me when she has problems or when there is no man in her life. Then she wants me to cheer her up. However, when I have a problem, she never has time for me. I don't want to lose her, but I'm feeling a bit used.

c) Your boyfriend's coldness could have several explanations – sexual jealousy, anger at betrayal of trust, embarrassment, or a mixture of all these. If your relationship is to have a future, he should give up his anger and forgive you. If he cannot forgive, you should accept that this relationship is finished.

d) I can understand why you feel so troubled. You are a married woman with a family and are happy with your life. If this man continues to follow you around, it could make your life very difficult. Why not explain your feelings to him? If you just think of him as a friend, but nothing more, he should know. Tell him you are happily married.

e) Solvent abuse is a growing problem. It caused 1,237 deaths between 1971 and 1991 and now kills three young people a week. Many of the substances which give a 'high', like lighter fuel and glue, are cheap and easily found in the home. You must talk to your son about this. If I were you, I would contact Re-Solv, the society for the prevention of solvent abuse, on 07850 817885 immediately.

f) Your feelings are quite understandable, but it is a risk you should be prepared to take. Why not ask your aunt to telephone your father first? It would be quite a shock for him to hear from you after so many years. Perhaps you could meet him and get to know him before you meet his family? Good luck!

4

Dear Helpline,

I'm terribly worried about my 15-year-old son. The happy-go-lucky boy I knew has become difficult and moody and disappears for hours with his mates, coming back worse than ever. At first I thought it was just his age, but I found a can of lighter fuel in his school bag and I am afraid he is now sniffing glue.

g) Have you thought about telling your friend how you feel? When she realises how her behaviour upsets you, she might change. If she doesn't change, you can decide if you want to finish the friendship. As we grow and change, friendships that worked well in the past don't always continue to be good for us.

5

Dear Helpline

I'm a secretary in a large company. My boss is so disorganised she never gives me the necessary information to write a report until the last minute. As a result, I have to work late at home or rush the job, which means it is badly done. This doesn't make me look good. What can I do?

Adapted from *Living* magazine

4

Your test: phrasal verbs puzzle

Make a list of sentences containing phrasal verbs you want to learn, and write each word on a different card, like this:

I	**can't**	**put**
up	**with**	**it.**

Now, for each sentence, write the meaning, or a more formal expression with the same meaning, on another card. Keep a list of your sentences and their meanings on a separate piece of paper.

Put all of the cards in a bag. The next day, pull out the cards, try to re-create the sentences, and then match them to their meanings. Use your paper with the list of sentences to check if you are correct.

Try again a week later, and then a month later.

1

Grammar: past progressive or past perfect tense

Read these extracts from someone telling the stories in Exercises 2 and 4, Unit 8 of the Coursebook. Make up appropriate responses using the past progressive or past perfect tense.

Example

A: Jack's neighbour thought he was getting an electric shock.
B: But in fact he (take off) *was taking off his boots.*

1 **A**: Jack's neighbour wanted to help him.
  B: But in fact he (misunderstand) _____
  _____

2 **A**: My friend's uncle was sitting with his head on the steering wheel.
  B: I see. He (fall asleep) _____
  _____

3 **A**: My friend's uncle escaped when two cars crashed.
  B: So he got away while the police (deal with)
  _____

4 **A**: The police car was in the garage with its blue light flashing.
  B: So your friend's uncle (take) _____
  _____

5 **A**: The old lady believed everything the friends told her and started filling the trolley.
  B: So she really thought that she (win) ____
  _____

6 **A**: The old lady hit the supermarket manager with the trolley.
  B: So he (try) _____
  _____

7 **A**: Kathy thought Ralph was her dream man.
  B: So she (never met) _____
  _____

8 **A**: When Ralph opened the door all he could see was mice. There was nothing else left.
  B: So the mice (eat) _____
  _____

2

Grammar: past progressive

Answer these questions truthfully about yourself last week. Use the past progressive tense.

Example
What were you doing at 8 am on Sunday?
I was eating breakfast.

What were you doing at …

1 9 am on Monday?
2 1 pm on Tuesday?
3 4 pm on Wednesday?
4 7 pm on Thursday?
5 10 pm on Friday?
6 8 am on Saturday?
7 3 pm on Saturday?
8 midnight on Saturday?
9 10 am on Sunday?
10 8 pm on Sunday?

3

Grammar: past perfect and past simple

Sometimes our dreams come true! Make true sentences about things which you always dreamed about which came true.

Example
I had always wanted to *go to India* and *when I was 19 I did.*

1 I had always wanted to _____
  and _____

2 I had always expected to _____
  but _____

3 I had never thought of _____ing _____
  but _____

4 I had always dreamt of _____ing _____
  and _____

5 I had always wanted a _____
  and _____

4
Intonation

Listen to the cassette and repeat the following. Try to copy the intonation you hear. Show that you are interested and want to hear more.

What happened then?   Whatever did you do?

Say these questions, then listen to the cassette and repeat.

1 What on earth did he do?   4 What happened next?

2 What did she say?   5 Where did it go?

3 How did it feel?   6 Who did you see?

5
Grammar: articles

Complete these quotations with 'a' or 'the' where necessary.

Example

'By all means marry; if you get *a* good wife, you'll be happy. If you get *a* bad one, you'll become *a* philosopher'. (**Socrates**)

a) 'Marrying (1) _____ man is like buying (2) _____ something you've been admiring for (3) _____ long time in (4) _____ shop window. You may love it when you get it home, but it doesn't always go with (5) _____ everything else in (6) _____ house.' (**Jean Kerr**)

b) '(1) _____ wives are (2) _____ people who feel they don't dance enough.' (**Groucho Marx**)

c) 'I've only slept with (1) _____ men I've been married to. How many (2) _____ women can make that claim?' (**Elizabeth Taylor**)

d) 'For (1) _____ while we wondered whether to take (2) _____ vacation or get (3) _____ divorce. We decided that (4) _____ trip to (5) _____ Bermuda is over in two weeks, but (6) _____ divorce is something you always have.' (**Woody Allen**)

e) 'Take it from me – (1) _____ marriage isn't (2) _____ word, it's (3) _____ sentence.' (**King Vidor**)

f) 'If you want to sacrifice (1) _____ admiration of (2) _____ many men for (3) _____ criticism of one, go ahead, get married.' (**Katharine Hepburn**)

g) 'We would have broken up except for (1) _____ children. Who were (2) _____ children? Well, she and I were.' (**Mort Sahl**)

Listen to the cassette and check your answers.

6
Classroom English

On the cassette you will hear a teacher in a classroom. Decide whether the teacher is *checking* (C) to see if you have understood, *praising* you (P) for getting something right, or *signalling* (S) the start of a new part of the lesson. Listen and mark 'C', 'P' or 'S'.

1 Right.   6 Right.

2 OK?   7 Right?

3 Yes.   8 OK.

4 Good.   9 Yes.

5 Now.

Then listen to the cassette again and repeat.

7
Your test

Take a section from one of the texts for Unit 8 of the Coursebook, or another text which you have found. Write the section out, making one of the following changes.

1 Leave a blank for every fifth word, like this:

Well, he had arranged _____ trip to America. He _____ going for five months, _____ around, buying sports equipment _____ his company.

2 Alternatively, put every verb in the infinitive form and leave a blank, like this:

Well, he (arrange) _____ a trip to America. He (go) _____ for five months, travelling around, buying sports equipment for his company.

Put your test away for one week. Then try to fill it in on your own or with another student.

LISTENING PRACTICE 2

Expert advice

The following people want to call *'Expert Advice'*, a radio programme in which a doctor, a psychiatrist and a community counsellor give advice to people with different problems.

a

After two years of marriage, my wife has just told me she never wants to have children. I am devastated. I want a big family.

b

I love my mother very much, but she is now senile, bad-tempered and very difficult to care for. She's a widow and we have a family and full-time jobs.

c

Our teenage daughter is violent and abusive at home and lazy and rude at school. We don't know what to do with her.

d

My wife hits me a lot. In fact, she attacks me nearly every day. Last week she stabbed me with her scissors. I just don't know what to do!

Listen to the extracts from the radio programme. Which two people called the programme for advice?

How much did you understand while you were listening?

80–100%	Brilliant!
60–80%	Good!
40–60%	Try listening again.
0–40%	Listen again and look at the tapescript.

Look at Listening Practice 1, page 14, for ideas on other activities to do.

1
Grammar: reporting verbs

In addition to 'said', we can use other verbs to report what someone has said:

ask (for questions)
He asked (me) what the time was.

tell (followed by the person who is spoken to)
I told him what the time was.

call (followed by an adjective or noun to describe the person)
He called me stupid.

Complete this imaginary conversation between Ike and Yale with 'asked', 'told' or 'called'.

Ike: I don't understand what's happening any more. It's like my whole life is falling apart. First you (1) _____ me that Mary found me attractive.

Yale: Yes, that's what she (2) _____ me.

Ike: So I (3) _____ her to marry me.

Yale: And?

Ike: She (4) _____ me that she wouldn't marry me yet. I (5) _____ her what she thought of me and she (6) _____ me that she thought of me as the father of her child! I was so happy I nearly jumped out of the window.

Yale: And?

Ike: Then yesterday she (7) _____ me that she still loved you. I was shocked. I didn't know what to say.

Yale: What did you say?

Ike: I (8) _____ her a liar. I (9) _____ her a cheat and a liar.

Yale: Oh no.

Ike: Yeah. It was a mistake. She (10) _____ me so many names back I can't remember them all, and maybe some weren't English anyway, and then she left.

Yale: Did she (11) _____ you where she was going?

Ike: Yeah. To your apartment. Oh, if you see her, can you (12) _____ her for my key back, please, and my clarinet . . .

Listen to the cassette and check your answers.

2
Reading comprehension: conversational signals

Read this text about the way we take turns in conversation, about who speaks when. What do you expect it to contain? 'Extra' words which are not part of the text have been added. As you read find these 'extra' words and underline them (the first one has been done for you). These words make up two sentences.

Sara tried to befriend her old friend Steve's new wife, but the Betty never seemed to have anything to say. While Sara felt Betty didn't hold up aim her end of the conversation, Betty complained to Steve that Sara never of gave her a chance to talk.

Conversation is a turn-taking game. You this talk, then I talk, then you talk again exercise. One person starts talking when another is finished. That seems simple enough is.

But how do you know when I'm finished? Well, when I stop. But to how do you know when I'm stopping? When my voice gets softer, when help I start repeating myself, or when I slow down and leave a gap at the end.

In the midst of a conversation, you don't take time to learner puzzle this out. You sense become when I'm finished, and when our habits are similar, there's no problem aware. What you sense and what I feel are similar. But if our habits are different, you may start of to talk before I'm finished – in other words, interrupt – or fail to take your turn the when I am finished – leading me to observe way that you're not paying attention or have nothing to say.

That's what was happening sentences with Betty and Sara. The tiny pause for which Betty kept waiting and never occurred when Sara was around, because before it did, Sara sensed an awkward texts silence and kindly ended it by filling the gap with more are talk – hers. And when Betty did start to say something built, she tended to have what seemed to Sara like long pauses within her speech, giving Sara the up impression that Betty had finished when she had hardly we got started.

It's interesting that Betty, who expected relatively longer read pauses between turns, is British, and Sara, who expected relatively shorter pauses, more is American. On average, British speakers tend to expect longer efficiently pauses between turns than when Americans.

Betty often felt interrupted by Sara. But Betty we herself became an interrupter and found herself doing all the talking when she can met a visitor from predict Finland who expected longer pauses. And Sara had a hard time saying anything at all the when she met visitors from Latin America or Israel words.

Adapted from *That's Not What I Meant* by Deborah Tannen

3

Grammar: question tags

Question tags at the end of sentences usually have a falling intonation when we expect someone to agree with us, and occasionally a rising intonation when we are really not sure.

🔊 Listen to the cassette:

Ike's really silly, isn't he?
(We both know he's silly.)

🔊 Some people are talking about Yale, Ike and Mary. Listen to the sentences on the cassette and complete them with a question tag and falling intonation.

1 You've heard the latest about Ike _____

2 He's living with Mary _____

3 She and Yale were friends _____

4 Ike and Mary used to argue _____

5 Mary left Ike _____

6 Yale still loved her _____

7 Yale and Mary are back together again _____

8 Yale is going to get a divorce _____

9 Ike is still on his own _____

10 The three are friends again now _____

3

4

Intonation: telephone conversations

As in ordinary conversations, falling intonation and longer pauses are used on the telephone to show that the speaker has finished and wants to end the conversation.

🔊 Listen to the cassette and decide if the speaker wants to finish (F) or continue (C) the telephone conversation.

Example

| F | | Well, thank you very much for ringing. |

1 ☐ That's all my news. How about you?

2 ☐ That's interesting. Good.

3 ☐ Fine. Thank you.

4 ☐ Is there anything else?

5 ☐ Is there anything else?

6 ☐ I'm very grateful. Yes.

7 ☐ That just about covers everything, does it?

8 ☐ That just about covers everything, doesn't it?

5

Classroom English: reporting back

🔊 Here are some phrases for use when pairs or a group are reporting their discussion back to the whole class. Listen to the cassette.

Well, what our group thought was that more people should use public transport.

We discussed the topic and decided that the car causes too much environmental damage.

Our conclusions are that car use should be limited and that no new roads should be built.

We've come to the conclusion that people will never give up their cars.

I'm afraid we haven't been able to agree on what to do about the transport crisis.

Although we've talked about the problem, we still haven't finished.

Can we have five more minutes please?

Is it all right if we carry on after class and report back next lesson?

We think there are three points: firstly, people love their cars; secondly, car owners pay a lot of taxes; and thirdly, the freedom to own a car is a basic human right right.

6

Your test

This is best done with a video but can be done with 'live' television. Choose a video of a film that you have seen and find a scene in it where two or three characters have a conversation. Play the video with the sound off and say the character's words. Don't worry if you can't remember what they actually said – just make up the words. If the video has an English sound-track, play the scene and see what the characters really said. Then try to 'act' the scene again yourself. If the video has sub-titles, cover them with a piece of paper over the bottom part of the screen. You may wish to make a tape recording of your 'acting'.

It is also very good to try out this activity with a friend or a small group of friends – in this case, each person can take the role of a different character.

1

Grammar: modals and question formation

a) Put these jumbled words into the right order to make questions.

Example

unborn child decide who happens what to should the

Who should decide what happens to the unborn child?

1 control is a genetic engineering get out of danger there that might

_____

2 genes we if change happen may what know do how we

_____

3 if information what I need I more must do

_____

4 responsibility genes person's a the who changing take should for

_____

5 doctors why us should tell what do to

_____

b) Make five similar jumbled questions yourself. Put them away and take them out in a few days, putting the words back into the right order.

2

Reading comprehension: question formation

Clinic to select baby's sex opens

Two doctors have opened Britain's first clinic which allows parents to choose the sex of their baby.

Using a technique developed in the United States, Dr Alan Rose and Dr Peter Liu are offering married couples who already have children an improved chance of having a baby of their chosen sex. Tests have shown that the technique has a 75 per cent success rate in producing boys and a 70 per cent success rate for girls. There are about 50 clinics using the technique in the US, but this is the first to be opened in Europe.

Carmel Turner, spokeswoman for the British Medical Association, said people should only be able to choose the sex of the child for medical reasons. "We think it's the thin edge of the wedge. It could be used by people who want a child of a particular sex for religious or cultural reasons."

Adapted from The Independent

a) Make questions about the text for these answers.

Example

How many doctors have opened the clinic?
Two.

1 _____?
Alan Rose and Peter Liu.

2 _____?
It allows parents to choose the sex of their baby.

3 _____?
Married couples with children.

4 _____?
75 per cent for boys and 70 per cent for girls.

5 _____?
Fifty.

6 _____?
She is a spokeswoman for the BMA.

7 _____?
She said people should only be able to choose their baby's sex for medical reasons.

b) Copy out the text, leaving out some of the words (perhaps every sixth word, or all the verbs – you choose). Listen to the text on the cassette and fill in the missing words.

c) 'We think it's the thin end of the wedge.' Which of the three objects in the picture is a wedge?

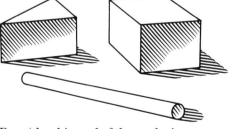

Does 'the thin end of the wedge' mean:

1 a good idea but one that won't work?

2 the beginning of a problem which will get much bigger?

3 the only thing that can be done?

3

Reading comprehension

Read the following arguments and decide if they are *for* or *against* selecting the sex of children. Write 'F' for *for* and 'A' for *against*.

The cases for and against sex selection

1 People should have as much choice over their lives as possible.

2 A child who is the 'right' sex would be greatly loved and valued.

3 Sex selection could place greater value on one sex than on the other.

4 If medical science offers a choice, people should have it.

5 Why is letting nature choose the sex of a child better than choosing yourself?

6 Paying for sex selection would make children like consumer goods.

7 A child should be valued for itself, not for its sex.

8 Sex is chosen by God. Humans shouldn't play God.

9 After sex selection we should be able to choose children's hair or eye colour.

10 Sex selection would upset nature's balance of male and female.

4

Pronunciation

a) Look at these words which are spelt differently but pronounced the same. Choose the correct word to complete each sentence.

Example

I must get a new pair of _jeans_.	genes/jeans	dʒiːnz
1 I'm so tired I really need a _____ .	break/brake	breɪk
2 The ship's _____ were damaged.	boughs/bows	baʊz
3 The _____ has already landed.	plain/plane	pleɪn
4 She _____ the volleyball.	threw/through	θruː
5 Can you please pass the _____?	bread/bred	bred
6 _____ discoveries are unquestioned.	some/sum	sʌm
7 '_____,' she said.	hi/high	haɪ
8 'I've got a headache,' he said with a _____ .	groan/grown	grəʊn
9 There is a danger of _____ on scientists.	a tax/attacks	ətæks

b) Word stress is emphasised when the speaker is expressing a strong opinion. Listen to the example on the cassette.

Example

It's barbaric!

Say these sentences in the same way, then listen and repeat.

1 It's ridiculous!

2 It's tremendous!

3 It's a breakthrough!

4 It's absurd!

5 It's unthinkable!

6 It's magnificent!

7 It's an impossible situation!

8 It's an important step!

9 It's wonderful!

10 It's exciting!

5

Classroom English: talking about pronunciation

Study this list of words used to talk about pronunciation and look at the examples.

consonant	b, c, d
vowel	a, e, o
syllable	words can be divided into syllables: **man:** 1, **wa-ter:** 2, **im-por-tant:** 3
stress	a stress mark shows the stressed syllable: **vege'tarian**
intonation	the way in which words are stressed in sentences
phonetic alphabet	shows how words are pronounced

6

Your test

Go back through Unit 10 of the Coursebook and write out new or interesting words with more than one syllable. Mark the stress by putting ' before the stressed syllable.

Example

vege'tarian

Now check the words in your dictionary and see how many are correct. You may wish to save a copy of the list and repeat the test in a few days.

YOUTH SURVEY

In a recent survey 579 children, aged 7 to 11, were asked what they wanted to be when they grew up. We expected to find girls wanting to do 'male' jobs. However, the answers were overwhelmingly traditional. Seventeen per cent of the girls wanted to be nurses, 10 per cent to be hairdressers and 9 per cent teachers. Others wanted to be vets, air hostesses, secretaries, shop assistants and pop singers. Although one girl wanted to be an engineer, none hoped to go into the fire brigade, the space industry or the armed forces. While 10 per cent of the girls liked the idea of working with children or babies, none of the boys did.

Adapted from The Independent

1

Grammar: conjunctions and connectors

Read these three newspaper extracts about the position of women at work. Complete the third one by choosing from this list:

although
however
nevertheless
on the one hand
on the other hand
while

Women at work in Britain
JOB FACTS

- **Just over three per cent of university professors are women.**

- **Only one per cent of secondary school heads are women. Nevertheless they make up 60 per cent of teacher numbers.**

- **Four per cent of senior managers in business are women.**

- **Women account for only eight per cent of architects.**

- **On the one hand, Parliament has a shooting club but, on the other, no nursery for children.**

Girls on top

(1) _____ 'Job Facts' makes depressing reading, recent surveys show that in the nineties girls are doing much better than boys in school examinations in all subjects, including mathematics and science.

A new report shows that (2) _____ 79% of women aged 18–34 want to develop their careers and (3) _____ only 50% see having children as an aim. Men still dominate the law. (4) _____, 54% of all new lawyers in Britain are women.

Twenty-five years ago 70% of university students were men. (5) _____ now as many women as men go to university.

2

Grammar: prepositions of time

a) Look at the following examples of uses of prepositions of time, and complete the rules.

1 **at**: at midnight, at one o'clock, at this moment, at New Year

   Rule: 'At' is used to show an _____ (exact/approximate) point of time and with festivals.

2 **in**: in 1999, in the summer, in June, in the morning/evening/afternoon (but **at** night), in an hour, in six months' time

   Rule: 'In' is used with _____ , _____ and _____ , with parts of the _____ , and to show a period when something will happen.

3 **by**: by the time he arrives, by next year, by Christmas

   Rule: 'By' indicates a limit to the time during which something _____ happen.

4 **for**: I've been here for an hour, I'm going away for a week

   Rule: 'For' is used to show a _____ (period/point of time).

5 **since**: I've been here since 6 pm, I've worked here since 1994

   Rule: 'Since' is used to show the _____ (start/end) of a period in the past.

6 **on**: on June 9th, on Friday

   Rule: 'On' is used with _____ and _____ .

b) Complete the following text with the correct prepositions of time.

When I lived in Egypt I used to get up (1) _____ 6.00 (2) _____ the morning and walk to work (3) _____ 7.00. (4) _____ the time I got to work it was 7.30. (5) _____ the winter we started work a little later. (6) _____ Friday there was no work. After working (7) _____ six hours I stopped (8) _____ 1.30 for lunch. As I had had nothing to eat (9) _____ breakfast, I was always hungry. Work started again (10) _____ the afternoon (11) _____ 4.00 and we worked (12) _____ another three hours.

3

Practical English: booking a hotel room

Read through these telephone conversations between hotel staff and someone who wants to book a room. Choose the best expression at each number.

A: Good morning. Grand Hotel.

B: Hello, I'd like to book a room for the nights of the …

A: Just a moment, please.

B: I'd like to book a room for the nights of the …

A: Just putting you through …

B: … of the 18th and 19th. Do you have any rooms?

A: This is the (1) switch/switchboard/exchange, sir. I'll put you through to (2) reservations/the booking office/room service.

B: Oh, thank you.

C: Good morning. Tomas Eklund. How can I help you?

B: I'd like to book a room for the nights of the 18th and 19th of this month please.

C: Certainly, sir. Just a moment and I'll (3) research/check/enquire availability. Is it a single or a (4) double/pair/duo?

B: A single. Do all the rooms have private (5) toilets/conveniences/bathrooms?

C: Yes, they do, sir. I'm afraid we're fully (6) charged/booked/ordered on the 18th.

B: How about the 19th and 20th?

C: Yes, we still have some (7) accommodations/chambers/vacancies then. The room (8) rate/charge/expense is 1290 Swedish crowns a night with Scandinavian breakfast buffet. That is (9) excluding/excepting/exceeding taxes of 12 per cent. Would you like to make a reservation?

B: Yes, please.

C: And will you be paying by credit card?

B: Yes.

C: Could you give me the full name as it appears on the card, please, and the number of the card and the (10) today's/exact/expiry date?

4

Pronunciation: strong and weak forms of prepositions

In some cases, a preposition can be pronounced in two ways: in a strong form when it is pronounced as it is written, and in a weak form when it is said more quickly and quietly.

a) Listen and repeat the strong form of each preposition followed by the weak form in a phrase.

Strong	Weak
at	at last
for	for lunch
in	in a box
on	on the table
to	to bed

b) Listen to these sentences and choose 'S' for *strong* and 'W' for *weak* forms of the prepositions.

Example

What time does it begin **at**? [S]

1 I've worked here **for** 12 years. [ ]

2 How long have you worked here **for**? [ ]

3 What day are you leaving **on**? [ ]

4 I'm leaving **on** Friday. [ ]

5 Which hotel is she staying **in**? [ ]

6 **At** two this afternoon. [ ]

7 I left it **in** the car. [ ]

8 It's ten **to** five. [ ]

c) Can you make up a rule to say when the prepositions in 4(a) have strong forms?

5

Classroom English: polite requests

Match the two halves of these sentences to make polite ways of asking about things in class.

1	Do you mind if	a)	to finish now. Is that OK?
2	Is it all right	b)	I leave ten minutes early?
3	Can I	c)	open a window, please?
4	We'd like	d)	if we don't complete all of it?

Listen to the cassette and check your answers.

6

Your test

a) Choose a text and copy it out, leaving out all the prepositions. Put the text away and the next day go through it, writing in the prepositions.

b) Make up sentences using the prepositions of time from Exercise 2, and write them out without the prepositions. After a few days fill in the prepositions.

1

Grammar: the passive

Body language is different in different cultures. Complete this text about Japan by putting the underlined verbs into the present simple (active or passive).

Non-verbal communication in Japan

Smile, laugh, giggle

Why the Japanese always (1) smile instead of saying yes or no? Why they (2) laugh when it (3) not be funny?

These questions often (4) ask by foreigners. The Japanese (5) laugh for many reasons, not only when they (6) amuse. They laugh when they (7) embarrass or (8) not be sure of what to say. A common reason for the Japanese to smile (9) be not wanting to say no. A smile (10) use to avoid hurting someone's feelings.

Avoidance of eye contact

The Japanese (11) try to avoid eye contact. It (12) not mean honesty or openness to them. On the contrary, eye contact (13) see as a challenge or threat. It (14) consider to be very impolite to maintain direct eye contact with someone whose status (15) be higher than yours. Japanese salesmen (16) teach to look at the customer's tie, not at the face.

Counting with the fingers

The fingers (17) use for counting in Japan in exactly the opposite way to the way of counting in Europe. They (18) start with the open hand and the fingers (19) fold in one by one, starting with the thumb. After five the fingers (20) open out again, starting with the little finger. This way of counting (21) learn quite easily.

Adapted from *Culture Shock! Japan* by Rex Shelley

2

Vocabulary: body movements

Complete the following text using these verbs, changing the form where necessary.

blow	scratch	suck
cover	sneeze	touch
rub	stroke	

Visitors to China are told not to (1) _____ their nose in public as this may offend people. It's easy to forget such advice and this happened to me on my first visit. It was very hot and dusty and dust got up my nose. I knew I was going to (2) _____ . So I took out my handkerchief. Then I remembered the advice, so I used the handkerchief to (3) _____ the dust from my hands. My nose still itched and I still wanted to (4) _____ . I didn't know what to do. I (5) _____ my nose with my left hand so no one could see and (6) _____ it with my fingernail. No good. I tried (7) _____ing a sweet but it didn't help. I tried (8) _____ing my nose gently with my fingers. Still no good – every time I (9) _____ my nose the itch got worse. In the end I asked to go to the toilet. Finally I was alone. I took out the handkerchief. But the itch had gone!

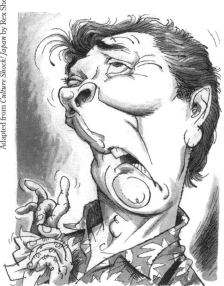

3

Word building: prefixes and suffixes

'<u>Un</u>certainty or doubt is indicated by scratching the side of the head …'
'It is a sign that the person is <u>un</u>happy.'

These examples from the text in Exercise 2 of the
Coursebook show how easy it is to change the meaning
of words by adding letters to the beginning or end.

Negative prefixes: 'un-' and 'dis-'

The meaning of a word can be changed by a prefix
(letters put at the start of the word).

Example

truth   untruth

a) Two common negative prefixes are 'un-' and 'dis-'.
Which of these two prefixes go with these words?

agree	equal	obey
appear	honest	satisfied
believe	kind	trust
comfortable	like	

Adjective suffixes: '-ish' and '-able'

Words can also be changed by suffixes (letters added to
the end of the word). Two common suffixes are '-ish'
and '-able'. The suffix '-ish' is added to a noun or
adjective to create an adjective and means 'being more
or less like'.

Example

brown   brownish (fairly brown)

The suffix '-able' is often added to a noun or verb to
create an adjective and means 'able to be'.

Example

understand   understandable (can be understood)

Note: there are some spelling changes.

Example

red   reddish
value   valuable

b) Make adjectives from these words by adding '-ish'
or '-able'.

work	do	teach
change	strong	amateur
boy	self	tiger
poor	long	believe
green	black	grey
reason	short	new
respect	think	old
fix	use	

4

Pronunciation: strong and weak forms of 'and' and 'but'

a) Listen and repeat the strong and weak forms.

Strong	Weak
and	fish and chips
	Mr and Mrs Palmer
but	sad but true
	But why?

b) Listen to the pronunciation of 'and' and 'but' in these
sentences and write 'S' for *strong* or 'W' for *weak*.

☐ 1 There's a Laurel and Hardy film on TV.

☐ 2 But it's time to go.

☐ 3 And I want to go.

☐ 4 I know, but I want to watch the end.

☐ 5 You go and I'll stay.

☐ 6 All right, but how will you get there?

☐ 7 I don't know, but I won't be late.

☐ 8 Don't forget the flowers! And the wine!

☐ 9 You take the wine and I'll bring the flowers.

☐ 10 Goodbye and enjoy the film!

5

Classroom English: correcting the teacher

There are times in every class when the teacher
mishears or makes a mistake. Use these sentences
to explain in a polite way that you think there is a
mistake. Match the two halves to make the sentences.

1 Excuse me, I didn't say
2 I beg your pardon, I
3 I'm terribly sorry, but isn't
4 I may be wrong,
5 I'm probably wrong about this,
6 Excuse me, there's a bit of a

a) problem. We don't know what to do.
b) it time to finish now?
c) 'bed', I said 'bid'.
d) but isn't the answer 'yes'?
e) thought you wanted us to start.
f) I thought you said page 30.

Listen to the cassette and check your answers.

6

Your test

Being able to predict how sentences will develop is an
important skill. To test yourself, all you need is a text
and a piece of card about the size of a postcard. Read
down the page line by line with the card covering the
line below. At the end of each line, guess what the first
words on the next line will be.

LISTENING PRACTICE 3

Dragon boss from hell

Offex (International) Ltd

Memo

Harassment Workshop for all staff:

The half-day workshop on harassment will be held on the morning of 13th September in room B41. Please note, the management requires **all** employees to attend this workshop on harassment.

Carol Ball
Training & Human Resources Dept

Listen to Pam, Teresa, Eric and Gordon discussing harassment in their group.

a) Which types of harassment have they experienced?

1 bullying behaviour by their boss

2 inappropriate remarks by their boss

3 inappropriate physical contact from their boss

b) They all agree that:

1 their boss is a bully, but he doesn't mean to be

2 their boss isn't a bully; he just has a bad management style

3 their boss is a bully and something needs to be done

c) How much did you understand while you were listening?

80–100% Brilliant!

60–80% Good!

40–60% Try listening again.

0–40% Listen again and look at the tapescript.

d) Look at Listening Practice 1 on page 14 for ideas on other activities to do.

Some employees of Offex (International) Ltd are attending the workshop on harassment.

Before listening, check that you understand the definition of harassment below. Use a dictionary to help you.

Harassment in the workplace

The term *harassment* is used to describe ways of behaving that are not acceptable or cause offence, for example, making rude or personal remarks, touching people in inappropriate ways, bullying or making people feel small or threatened. *Harassment* can make the workplace uncomfortable and intimidating. If you *feel* that you are being harassed, then you are, even if the harasser is not doing it on purpose.

1
Grammar: passive with modals

The passive form of the infinitive ('be' + past participle) is used after modal verbs ('can', 'have to', 'may', 'might', 'must', 'need to', 'will', 'should') and also after 'going to', 'want to' and 'would like to'.

a) Rewrite these sentences putting them into the passive.

Example
You must respect the name card.
The name card must be respected.

1 You must treat name cards like the people themselves.

2 One should present the name card with two hands and a bow.

3 You must give the company name first, then your own.

4 The giver should hold the card so that the receiver can read it.

5 You must look at a card when someone gives it to you.

6 We will print the cards in English and Japanese.

7 They are going to hold a meeting about the new factory tomorrow.

8 Someone might misunderstand your meaning.

9 You need to explain clearly exactly what has to be done.

b) Write out in full these instructions at a car-wash, using 'must' (m) and 'should' (s).

Example
Protective clothing/wear (m)
Protective clothing must be worn.

1 engine/turn off (m)

2 windows/close (m)

3 windscreen wipers/fix (s)

4 coins/insert in the slot (s)

5 programme required/select (s)

6 car/drive forward (s)

7 brakes/apply (s)

8 engine/start/after the end of the wash (s)

9 car/drive out/at once (s)

2
Listening: life in Japan

a) Listen to this advice to foreigners about how to live cheaply in Japan and find out the following information.

1 the price of a fast train ticket from Narita Airport to Tokyo

2 the name of a reasonably priced restaurant

3 a cheap way to get from Tokyo to Kyoto

4 an easy way to save money on household goods

b) Listen to this description of meetings in Japan and fill in the missing words.

Foreigners usually misunderstand the way business or office meetings work in Japan. In fact, when they work well, the Japanese way of (1) _____ meetings is really good – and far better than what we (2) _____ to in the West. I lived in Japan for a couple of years and at the start I couldn't work (3) _____ what was happening at meetings – they used to go (4) _____ for hours and hours but no decisions were (5) _____ . The first thing that has to (6) _____ is that decisions are not taken at Japanese meetings. The decisions (7) _____ before the meeting, and the purpose of the meeting is for everyone (8) _____ to the decision. Of course, decisions aren't taken (9) _____ asking people what they think, but this happens (10) _____ the meeting. You (11) _____ your opinion and can express your views before the meeting takes place. (12) _____ you say is considered carefully and a decision is taken. Then a meeting (13) _____ and the decision is (14) _____ by everyone – the decision is now something which everyone 'owns'.

Listen to the cassette again and check your answers.

3
Vocabulary: shape and position

Match these expressions and drawings.

1 upside-down
2 right way up
3 side by side
4 inside-out
5 back to front
6 one on top of the other
7 in the top right-hand corner
8 in the bottom left-hand corner
9 sideways
10 backwards
11 forwards

4
Pronunciation: word stress

In some words the position of the stress changes the meaning. For example, 'present' is a noun meaning a gift, 'pres'ent' is a verb meaning give formally.

Listen to the pronunciation on the cassette:

Just before you present your card . . .

I've brought a present for you.

Look at the underlined words in each pair of sentences. Listen to the cassette and mark the stress to show which word you hear.

1 a) When you leave the company they will present you with a gold watch.
   b) I was given a gold watch as a present.

2 a) The object of the meeting is to get everyone to agree.
   b) Do you object to what is suggested?

3 a) Our company imports cloth.
   b) The government wants to tax cloth imports.

4 a) We want to export more goods.
   b) This is export quality.

5 a) The machine rejects low-quality goods.
   b) These are low-quality rejects.

5
Classroom English: correcting

It is not always easy to see your own mistakes in written work. A good way of working is to exchange written work with a partner. However, instead of correcting any mistakes you find, try underlining the mistake and putting a symbol in the margin to tell your partner what kind of mistake it is. Going through your own corrected written work and writing symbols in the margin will show you where you are making most mistakes.

Example

t   I'm going to London yesterday.

Here 't' is the symbol for 'tense'.

Try using the following symbols or make up your own.

t	tense
sp	spelling
punct	punctuation
prep	preposition
wo	word order
wm	word missing
v	vocabulary
st	style

Look through your own written work and see if any more symbols are needed.

6
Your test

Take a text in English which you haven't read before and write it out by hand or on a computer without any punctuation, capital letters or spaces between the words or paragraphs. Keep the text and your version of it for a week. Then go through your version and try and re-create the original text. Note any mistakes you have made.

If this is very difficult, use a text which you know from this book. If it is very easy, try choosing a range of different texts (e.g. advertisements, the words of songs, technical instructions, stories).

1

Grammar: present perfect passive

Refer to the text on the Italian floods in Exercise 4(a) of the Coursebook, and imagine you are a journalist. You have been sent to Italy one year after the floods. You have a list of the topics you want to check on. Write one sentence about each topic, choosing one of the verbs and using the information given after the topic.

Example

Topic: victims (not all)　　**Verb**: compensate
Sentence: Not all the victims have been compensated.

Topics

		Verbs	
1 Houses (some)	5 Crops (some)	compensate	restore
2 Electrical supplies (all)	6 Rivers (few)	control	rehouse
3 People (most)	7 Victims (not all)	rebuild	reopen
4 Roads (all)	8 Damage (most)	repair	replant

2

Grammar: past simple and past perfect passive

A year after the floods a newspaper report described what happened. Put the verbs in the correct tense using the past simple, past simple passive and past perfect passive.

So, one year on, what really happened? Although heavy rain (1) _____ (forecast) for several days, no one (2) _____ (prepare) for the downpour which finally (3) _____ (come). The worst of the rain (4) _____ (expect) on the coast but in fact it (5) _____ (fall) in the mountains. This (6) _____ (make) the floods much worse. Large areas of mountainside (7) _____ (clear) of trees over the previous few years so the rainfall (8) _____ (pour) down into the valleys which soon (9) _____ (flood). The rivers (10) _____ (can) not cope with the volume of water and (11) _____ (break) their banks. Soon all the fields (12) _____ (cover) in deep water and whole villages (13) _____ (wash) away.

Plans (14) _____ (make) many years before for a flood disaster like this but no one could have expected so much rain in such a short period. The authorities cannot (15) _____ (blame) for the disaster and should (16) _____ (praise) for their reaction to it.

3

Listening: the sub-editor's job

a) Listen to a sub-editor on a major British newspaper describing her job. Listen without stopping for overall understanding, then listen again, stopping and replaying where necessary to get more detail.

b) Listen again, stopping where necessary, in order to complete this diagram.

Listen again and follow the tapescript to check your answers.

1 Stories are typed into the system by _____ .

2 Stories are _____ and assessed for their news value.

3 Sub-editor has 3 main concerns:
a _____ y
cl_____ y
p _____ tion

4 Sub-editor has to _____ the stories to _____ the page.

5 When all the stories _____ the page, it is typeset.

4

Vocabulary: the weather

Put the words listed below into these four categories :

Sun	Water	Snow and ice	Wind

blizzard	downpour	fog	heat wave
breeze	drizzle	frost	hurricane
cloudburst	drought	gale	mist
dew	flood	hail	sleet

5

Pronunciation: countries and nationalities

In Unit 1 we looked at countries and nationalities, and how to pronounce them. Most nationality adjectives are formed by adding the following suffixes:

'-an/-ian'   '-ish'   '-ese'   '-i'

Adding the suffix can change the stress.

Example

'Egypt	–	E'gyptian
'Italy	–	I'talian

In other cases there is no change.

Example

'India	–	'Indian

Form nationality adjectives for these countries and group them according to the suffix used. Mark the stress and say if the nationality has the *same* stress as the country (S) or a *different* stress (D).

Algeria	Saudi Arabia
Israel	South Africa
Kenya	Syria
Kuwait	Tunisia
Lebanon	Turkey
Morocco	
Argentina	Cuba
Bolivia	Jamaica
Brazil	Mexico
Canada	Peru *(careful!)*
Chile	Venezuela
Colombia	
Australia	Nepal
Bangladesh	Korea
China	Pakistan
Indonesia	Taiwan
Japan	Thailand *(careful!)*
Malaysia	Vietnam

Listen to the cassette and check your answers.

6

Classroom English: definitions

It is very unusual for two words to mean exactly the same. So when you ask someone about a word (for example, 'What does "sleet" mean?'), they are likely to explain by a definition rather than a word ('It's a kind of wet snow – a sort of mixture of rain and snow').

Complete each of these sentences with a word and its definition.

1 _____ is an informal expression meaning

_____

2 A person who _____

   is a _____

3 _____ is a kind of _____

   It's a bit _____

4 When you're _____ you are _____

5 A _____ is someone who _____

   _____

6 Something which is _____ is _____

   _____

Words	Definitions
drizzle	completely wet
pouring down	fine rain like spray
soaking	isn't killed in an accident
survivor	raining very hard
tragic	is attacked or killed
victim	very sad

7

Your test

Take any English language newspaper and cut out as many articles as you can, including the headlines. Turn each article over and write the headline on the back. Then cut off the headline. Put the articles in one pile and the head-lines in another.

Look at the articles and try to make up a headline for each one. Then go through the pile of headlines and match the headlines and articles.

1

Grammar: future passive and future perfect passive

Use verb phrases from the list to complete these sentences about the world in 50 years' time. The sentences can be positive or negative.

Examples

Trains/drive automatically
Trains will be driven automatically.

Poverty/wiped out
Poverty will not have been wiped out.

1 Computers _____

2 Typhoid _____

3 Holidays _____

4 Cars _____

5 Marriage _____

6 Children _____

7 Work _____

8 Books _____

Verb phrases

make illegal	become unnecessary
wipe out	allow in towns
abolish	make compulsory
educate at home	become very cheap

2

Grammar: reported speech

Here is a list of predictions made over a hundred years ago. Put them into reported speech and mark them 'R' (right) or 'W' (wrong).

Example

We hope smallpox will be wiped out.
They hoped that smallpox would be wiped out.   R

1 We believe every person will be free.

2 We think balloons will be the air transport of the future.

3 We expect there will be enough food for everyone.

4 We are sure women will not be given the vote.

5 We think children will leave school at ten.

6 We expect there will be no more wars.

7 We think French will be the world language.

8 We think electric trains will be invented.

9 We hope people will travel in space.

10 We are sure there will be political prisoners.

3

Reading: a world without books

Use spaces, punctuation and capital letters to recreate this text.

> **CLOSE THE BOOK!**
>
> By2020havingaroomfulofbookswill showyoutobeoldfashionedmajorworksof referencewillgofirstnoonebuys encyclopediasanymorebecauseitisfar easiertosearchforinformationonacdrom butasscreensbecomelighterandbrighter andcanhavethethicknessandsizeofa magazinetheelectronicbookwillreplace thenoveltheadvantagesarethatyoucan storehundredsofbooksordownload themfromaterminalwithaconnectionto thepublisherinsteadofgoingtoabook shopyou'llbeabletosampleasmanybooks asyoulikeelectronicallyandtakethewhole bookonlyifyouwantit

Adapted from New Scientist

4

Vocabulary: phrasal verbs with 'over' and 'out'

Add 'over' or 'out' to the verbs to form phrasal verbs which complete the sentences.

Examples

wipe No one will suffer from the disease. It will be *wiped out*.

take CDs have replaced records in most countries. They have *taken over* from records and cassettes.

Verbs

break	hand	think
burst	put	wear
go	talk	

1 All-out war may be near. Fighting has _____ _____ between rival groups in the capital city.

2 It was late at night. The room became colder and colder. It was dark. Then I noticed that the fire had _____ _____ .

3 She suddenly saw the joke and _____ _____ laughing.

4 We can't just take a decision without discussion. I'd like to _____ things _____ .

5 This is a No Smoking area. Please _____ _____ your cigarette.

6 This old coat is completely _____ _____ .

7 There's a lot to consider in these papers. I'd like time to _____ things _____ .

8 The policeman asked him to _____ _____ the stolen goods.

5

Pronunciation

'We predicted that there would be enough food.' Which word in this sentence rhymes with 'wood'? The answer is 'would'. 'Food' has a longer sound like 'too' and 'new'.

Find the odd word out in these lists.

1 could   should   rude   good

2 bed   paid   said   wed

3 made   paid   said   stayed

4 read (present tense)   dead   need   feed

5 read (past tense)   red   lead (metal)   lead (go in front)

6 force   course   horse   worse

7 divorce   worse   verse   nurse

▶ Listen to the cassette and check your answers.

6

Classroom English: feedback

When you are evaluating your own progress or performance, or giving feedback to another student or the teacher, it is important to be clear. Practise the language needed by completing these sentences about either this unit or your whole course.

1 I found _____ing _____ very worthwhile.

2 It was always useful when we _____

3 It would have been better if we _____

4 I feel that we could have spent more time _____ing _____

5 It would have been useful to _____

6 I think that _____ing _____ was something we could have done more of.

7 There should have been more _____

8 It would have been nice if _____

9 _____ has been absolutely wonderful!

7

Your test

Go back through this book and find the tests which you made up for Units 1–14. Do the tests again and see how much you remember. Exchange tests with other students and see how you get on with theirs.

1

Grammar: future progressive and future perfect

Complete the dialogue by putting the verbs into the future progressive ('will be' + '-ing') or future perfect ('will have' + past participle).

Examples

A: Do you think language teaching methods (change) *will have changed* much by 2020?

B: No, I expect people (still learn) *will still be learning* in the same old way.

A: I'm not sure about that. I think that a lot of things (1 change) _____ . More and more people (2 work) _____ at home and technology (3 develop) _____ so that they will be able to study without being in a class with a teacher.

B: Without a teacher? What (4 happen) _____ to all the teachers?

A: I didn't say 'without a teacher', I said 'without being in a class with a teacher'. All over the world people (5 learn) _____ languages at home using interactive technology.

B: What's that?

A: Computers which are linked to each other and to a central point. Computers (6 become) _____ so cheap and powerful by then that a good computer program and one teacher will be able to work with hundreds of students.

B: So what they (7 do) _____ that is so different from now?

A: They (8 learn) _____ at their own speed and in their own time. Computer programs (9 be developed) _____ to enable learners to personalise their learning.

B: A bit like 'It's your choice!'?

A: Yes. And learners will still talk to the teacher, and see her, using two-way video.

B: Great! There's just one problem, though. I'm making so much progress that I don't think I (10 still study) _____ English in 2020!

3

Your future English language learning

Learning without a teacher or textbook can be fun and effective. Think about your own situation and look back through this book, and then copy and complete the following list.

Ways in which I can practise speaking

_____

Ways in which I can improve my listening

_____

Ways in which I can improve my reading and writing

_____

Ways of increasing my vocabulary

_____

Ways of improving my grammatical accuracy

_____

2

Grammar: future progressive

The future progressive is often used when we make polite requests, or ask a polite question about someone's plans.

Examples

Will you be using your computer tonight? (= If not, can I use it?)

Will you be working late again tonight? (Much more polite than 'Are you working late?' or 'Are you going to work late?')

Make questions using the future progressive which fit these situations.

1 You want to use the car tomorrow night. Ask your friend.

2 You want to know if your friend is going to the party on Saturday.

3 You want to know if your friend is getting a birthday present for Sue.

4 You want to wear your friend's red coat tomorrow.

5 You want to know if your friend is going to the football match.

4

Listening: the Carioca goodbye

Think back to Exercise 2 about Carioca body language in Unit 1 of the Coursebook. How do you think Cariocas say goodbye?

Listen to the description on the cassette. Then listen again and fill in the missing words.

Cariocas, (1) _____ nature, (2) _____ to be (3) _____ open, warm and friendly. And (4) _____ show (5) _____ friendliness, you can be (6) _____ that they (7) _____ say farewell (8) _____ a simple 'goodbye'. It would be just (9) _____ dry and not (10) _____ keeping (11) _____ their nature. (12) _____ you want to behave (13) _____ a real Carioca, (14) _____ end a conversation (15) _____ one of the following:

1 "A gente se ve": (16) _____
2 "Te ligo": (17) _____ you.
3 "Aparece em casa": Show (18) _____ at my (19) _____ at any time.
(20) _____ remember! These phrases are (21) _____ to be taken (22) _____ . In other words, they (23) _____ :
1 "We (24) _____ be seeing each other (25) _____ soon."
2 "(26) _____ wait for my (27) _____ call."
3 "(28) _____ show (29) _____ at my (30) _____ ."

Adapted from *How to be a Carioca* by Priscilla Ann Goslin

5

How to say goodbye

a) In the first exercise of Coursebook Unit 1 we heard people greeting each other in different languages on the beach in Rio. Here are the same people saying farewell. Can you recognise who is who? Number the languages to show the order of the speakers.

Arabic   French   Italian   Japanese
Chinese   German   Portuguese   Spanish
English

b) Listen to these ways of saying goodbye in English to someone you have just met. Number them as follows:

a) very formal   b) neutral   c) friendly   d) very friendly

1 It's been a great pleasure to make your acquaintance.

2 I've really loved meeting you. It's been wonderful.

3 It was good to get to know you.

4 I enjoyed meeting you very much.

6

Pronunciation: friendly goodbyes

Using a rising intonation and making the words longer are a common way of saying a very friendly goodbye – perhaps to friends we won't see again for a while or after a pleasant evening or party.

Practise saying these farewells in a friendly way, and then listen to the cassette and repeat.

1 Goodbye.
2 Cheerio!
3 See you!
4 Take care now.
5 Look after yourself!
6 See you soon, I hope.
7 Bye bye!
8 Cheers!

7

Classroom English: the language of reports

Reports at the end of a course are an important form of feedback but students often ask what some of the phrases mean. So here is a small glossary explaining (not entirely seriously!) the meaning of commonly used report phrases.

Report phrase	Meaning?
She shows promise	She doesn't do any work but would be good if she did.
Participates well in class	Shouts out all the time
Interacts well with other students	Never stops talking
Works steadily at his own speed	is always asleep
Has her own priorities	Never comes to class
Able to take the initiative	Asked the teacher for a date
Enthusiastic	Sits at the front
Hard-working	Never finishes anything
A lively participant	Brought a gun to class
Model student	Father is important politician
Could try harder	Stop listening to walkman
Could try much harder	Stop using mobile phone
Always pays attention	Sits and stares at the teacher
Always punctual	Does he live in the classroom?
Top of the class	Used to live in USA and criticises the teacher's English

8

Your test: remembering the book

This is a test which you can do any time, anywhere: in the shower, on the bus or on the beach. Close your eyes and think of a unit in the book. Remember everything you can about the unit: the pictures, the texts, the activities, the listening. Try to think in English and go through the unit in your head. It's a wonderful way of reviewing. Try doing one unit a day!

LISTENING PRACTICE 4

Immortality for £23,000!

Immortality for £23,000!

Cryonic future for Derby family

We'll live again in the future!
The Blackman family have decided to be frozen

Family on ice

Listen to an extract from the radio programme in which the Blackman family discuss their decision to be frozen when they die.

Say whether the following statements are true or false.

a) All the members of the Blackman family have agreed to be frozen when they die.

b) Bob Blackman thinks that, by the time he is revived, it will also be possible to rejuvenate frozen people.

c) Paula Blackman would like to have more children when she is revived in the future.

d) Before you are frozen, all your blood is removed from your body and replaced with a kind of anti-freeze.

e) Your head is the last part to be frozen.

f) The frozen bodies will be shipped to Michigan and stored.

g) The most exciting thing for Max is to see what the future is like.

h) Emily doesn't want to be treated like a freak in the future.

i) Emily doesn't know how she will react when her parents die.

j) Emily thinks that you can't revive a frozen person because their spirit will not be in their body.

k) Emily's parents want her to change her mind about being frozen.

l) Emily's father thinks it's very expensive to be frozen.

How much did you understand while you were listening?

80–100% Brilliant!

60–80% Good!

40–60% Try listening again.

0–40% Listen again and look at the tapescript.

Look at Listening Practice 1 on page 14 for ideas on other activities to do. Do you think your listening has improved since the start of this course?

ANSWER KEY

Unit 1 Exercise 1

a)
1 to follow	6 to be
2 showing	7 to pass
3 knowing	8 standing
4 introducing	9 making
5 meeting	10 stepping

b)
1 sitting
2 making
3 sitting
4 drinking
5 speaking

Unit 1 Exercise 2

1 I perform in plays	Theatre
2 I bring your food	Restaurant
3 I teach geography	Secondary school
4 I break in and steal	Your house
5 I make money	Office
6 I serve food on planes	Airline
7 I work for the government	Office
8 I input data	Office
9 I can use a gun	The army
10 I look after your teeth	Surgery
11 I design bridges	Office
12 I work in a shop	Shop
13 I write newspapers	Office
14 I run a shop	Shop
15 I repair cars	Garage
16 I play the violin	Orchestra
17 I care for the sick	Hospital
18 I study theory	University
19 I welcome you on arrival	Hotel
20 I type letters and answer the phone	Office

Unit 1 Exercise 3

1 ↗
2 ↗
3 ↘
4 ↘
5 ↗
6 ↘
7 ↗
8 ↘
9 ↗
10 ↗
11 ↗
12 ↘
13 ↘
14 ↗
15 ↘

Unit 1 Exercise 4

See Tapescript Unit 1 Exercise 4

Unit 2 Exercise 1

1 like speaking	5 would like to see
2 would like to talk	6 like teaching
3 would like to learn	7 would like to do
4 like learning	

Unit 2 Exercise 2

A microchip is something which controls a computer.
A comedian is someone who makes people laugh.
A teenager is someone who is between 13 and 19.
A 'green' is someone who cares about the environment.
A microwave is something which heats food.
A pensioner is someone who has retired.
A candidate is someone who is applying for a job.
A graduate is someone who has been to university.
A drop-out is someone who rejects society.

Unit 2 Exercise 3

interested	secretary
business	several
literature	average
comfortable	medicine
different	favourite
listening	vegetable
vocabulary	

Unit 3 Exercise 1

1 have	11 left	20 was
2 was	12 commenced	21 painted
3 have	13 went	22 was
4 live	14 say	23 painted
5 lives	15 hated	24 was
6 is	16 was	25 did
7 was	17 was	26 was
8 went	18 decided	27 was
9 went	19 wanted	28 had
10 went		

Unit 3 Exercise 4

1 Type A: cost, cost, cost   cut, cut, cut   hit, hit, hit
   let, let, let   put, put, put   shut, shut, shut
   set, set, set
2 Type B: get, got, got   lose, lost, lost
3 Type B: sell, sold, sold   tell, told, told
4 Type B: build, built, built   spend, spent, spent
5 Type B: bleed, bled, bled   feed, fed, fed
   hold, held, held   lead, led, led   read, read, read
   (Note: for 'read' the spelling stays the same but the
   pronunciation changes.)
6 No type! Here the verb and the past participle are the
   same: become, became, become
   come, came, come   run, ran, run
7 Type B: hear, heard, heard   make, made, made
   pay, paid, paid   say, said, said
8 Type B: dream, dreamt, dreamt   feel, felt, felt
   keep, kept, kept   leave, left, left
   mean, meant, meant   meet, met, met
   sleep, slept, slept
9 Type B: hang, hung, hung   win, won, won
10 Type C: begin, began, begun   drink, drank, drunk
   ring, rang, rung   sing, sang, sung   sink, sank, sunk
   swim, swam, swum
11 Type C: bite, bit, bitten   hide, hid, hidden
12 Type B: bring, brought, brought   buy, bought, bought
   fight, fought, fought   think, thought, thought
   catch, caught, caught   teach, taught, taught
13 Type C: break, broke, broken   choose, chose, chosen
   steal, stole, stolen
14 Type C: know, knew, known   grow, grew, grown
   throw, threw, thrown
15 Type C: shake, shook, shaken   take, took, taken
16 Type C: drive, drove, driven   ride, rode, ridden
   rise, rose, risen   write, wrote, written
17 Type C: eat, ate, eaten   fall, fell, fallen   do, did, done
   fly, flew, flown   forget, forgot, forgotten
   give, gave, given   go, went, gone   see, saw, seen

Unit 3 Exercise 5

1 A	14 B	27 A	40 A
2 B	15 B	28 B	41 B
3 B	16 C	29 C	42 A
4 C	17 C	30 B	43 B
5 C	18 A	31 C	44 B
6 B	19 B	32 A	45 A
7 B	20 C	33 A	46 B
8 B	21 B	34 C	47 C
9 C	22 B	35 B	48 A
10 B	23 A	36 B	49 C
11 C	24 B	37 C	50 B
12 A	25 C	38 B	51 C
13 B	26 B	39 C	52 B

Unit 3 Exercise 6

1 .	5 *	9 "	13 +
2 ,	6 =	10 "	14 ?
3 (	7 :	11 !	15 –
4)	8 ;	12 —	

Unit 4 Exercise 1

1 will	6 am going to
2 is not going to	7 am going to
3 is going to	8 will
4 is going to	9 will
5 will	10 will

Unit 4 Exercise 2

1 to have	6 to be
2 to do	7 to have
3 to live	8 to be
4 to own	9 to travel
5 to live	10 to seek

Unit 4 Exercise 3

a) A H J K
   B C D E G P T V
   F L M N S X Z*
   I Y
   O
   Q U W
   R

   * 'Z' has two pronunciations:

   British English – /zed/
   USA English – /ziː/

b) See Tapescript Unit 4 Exercise 3(b)

Unit 4 Exercise 4

1 I	6 I
2 Q	7 Q
3 Q	8 I
4 Q	9 I
5 I	10 I

Listening Practice 1

The most accurate summary is (c)

Unit 5 Exercise 1

a) 1 b)   4 f)
   2 d)   5 c)
   3 e)   6 a)

b) 1 e)   5 g)
   2 d)   6 a)
   3 h)   7 f)
   4 b)   8 c)

Unit 5 Exercise 2

Families around the world

The common image of the family in the West is the nuclear family: mother, father and two children. This image is no longer true of many Western societies where couples living together with no children (kids) are the largest group, and where families frequently break up. The average size of a family in 1900 was 4.6; now it is 2.51. In Britain, for example (just to take one case), one in five families have only one parent, and the global figure is between a quarter and a third of all families.

(You get a lot more) Extended families are much more common in other parts of the world. In extended families two or more generations – parents, grandmother and grandfather (gran and grandpa), and children – live together, sometimes with more distant relatives. Such extended families (Great big families like this) provide a support network that helps the children (kids) and old people (folks) to be looked after. It is most common (You get it a lot of it) in countries where a large family is vital as a source of labour.

The environment often influences the family. Polygamy, where a man (bloke) has more than one wife (missus), is often found where there is plenty of land and women produce much of the food, for example in southern Africa. Where (there isn't much) good land is scarce, polyandry, where a woman has more than one husband, is not uncommon (happens quite a lot). The Nyinba people of Nepal in the Himalayas practise fraternal polyandry, where the husbands are brothers. This limits (cuts down) family size and means that several men can support one family.

Unit 5 Exercise 3

a) 1 sneeze 4 pant   6 yawn
   2 cough   5 sigh   7 snore
   3 hiccup

b) 1 sheep   bleat
   2 cat   mew
   3 duck   quack
   4 horse   neigh
   5 snake   hiss
   6 cow   moo

Unit 5 Exercise 4

amusing apparently entertaining approach away finally supposed banana yoghurt correct magazine

Unit 5 Exercise 5

1 d)   6 j)
2 e)   7 b)
3 g)   8 i)
4 h)   9 f)
5 c)   10 a)

Unit 6 Exercise 1

b) 1 mine   8 what
   2 explain   9 cat
   3 course   10 Black
   4 why   11 yes
   5 dear   12 lied
   6 say   13 friend
   7 friend   14 white

Unit 6 Exercise 2

a) 1 a slow-moving car
   2 a quick-thinking person
   3 an angry-looking person
   4 an easy-going person
   5 a fun-loving person

b) 1 a hard-hearted person
   2 a quick-tempered person
   3 a brown-eyed person
   4 a bad-mannered person
   5 a long-haired person

Unit 6 Exercise 3

careful/careless
doubtful/doubtless
harmful/harmless
hopeful/hopeless
painful/painless
peaceful
powerful/powerless
priceless
skilful
speechless
thoughtful/thoughtless
youthful

Unit 6 Exercise 4

scientist chocolate written every people naturally fascinated mystery family friends fighter thumb thoughtful straightforward climb hour two know answer secretary half talk

Unit 6 Exercise 5

See Tapescript Unit 6 Exercise 5

Unit 7 Exercise 1

1 If I were you, I'd get a television. / I'd get a television if I were you.
2 If I were him, I would get a good grammar book. / I would get a good grammar book if I were him.
3 If I were her, I would go to the library to study. / I would go to the library to study if I were her.
4 If I were you, I would buy them some video cartoons in English. / I would buy them some video cartoons in English if I were you.
5 If I were you, I would write down new vocabulary ten times. / I would write down new vocabulary ten times if I were you.

Unit 7 Exercise 3

1 c)   4 e)
2 f)   5 b)
3 g)

Unit 8 Exercise 1

Suggested answers

1 But in fact he had misunderstood (the situation).
2 I see. He had fallen asleep.
3 So he got away while the police were dealing with the crash.
4 So your friend's uncle had taken the police car.
5 So she really thought that she had won a prize.
6 So he was trying to stop her.
7 So she never met anyone better.
8 So the mice had eaten everything.

Unit 8 Exercise 5

a) 1 a   4 a
   2 –   5 –
   3 a   6 the

b) 1 –   2 –

c) 1 the   2 –

d) 1 a   4 a
   2 a   5 –
   3 a   6 a

e) 1 –   3 a
   2 a

f) 1 the   3 the
   2 –

g) 1 the   2 the

Unit 8 Exercise 6

1 S   6 P
2 C   7 C
3 P   8 S
4 S   9 P
5 S

Listening Practice 2

(c) and (d)

Unit 9 Exercise 1

1 told   7 told
2 told   8 called
3 asked   9 called
4 told   10 called
5 asked 11 tell
6 told   12 ask

Unit 9 Exercise 2

Sara tried to befriend her old friend Steve's new wife, but the Betty never seemed to have anything to say. While Sara felt Betty didn't hold up aim her end of the conversation, Betty complained to Steve that Sara never of gave her a chance to talk.

Conversation is a turn-taking game. You this talk, then I talk, then you talk again exercise. One person starts talking when another is finished. That seems simple enough is.

But how do you know when I'm finished? Well, when I stop. But to how do you know when I'm stopping? When my voice gets softer, when help I start repeating myself, or when I slow down and leave a the gap at the end.

In the midst of a conversation, you don't take time to learner puzzle this out. You sense become when I'm finished, and when our habits are similar, there's no problem aware. What you sense and what I feel are similar. But if our habits are different, you may start of to talk before I'm finished – in other words, interrupt – or fail to take your turn the when I am finished – leading me to observe way that you're not paying attention or have nothing to say.

That's what was happening sentences with Betty and Sara. The tiny pause for which Betty kept waiting and never occurred when Sara was around, because before it did, Sara sensed an awkward texts silence and kindly ended it by filling the gap with more are talk – hers. And when Betty did start to say something built she tended t o have what seemed to Sara like long pauses within her speech, giving Sara the up impression that Betty had finished when she had hardly we got started.

It's interesting that Betty, who expected relatively longer read pauses between turns, is British, and Sara, who expected relatively shorter pauses, more is American. On average, British speakers tend to expect longer efficiently pauses between turns than when Americans.

Betty often felt interrupted by Sara. But Betty we herself became an interrupter and found herself doing all the talking when she can met a visitor from predict Finland who expected longer pauses. And Sara had a hard time saying anything at all the when she met visitors from Latin America or Israel words.

Unit 9 Exercise 3

1 You've heard the latest about Ike, haven't you?
2 He's living with Mary, isn't he?
3 She and Yale were friends, weren't they?
4 Ike and Mary used to argue, didn't they?
5 Mary left Ike, didn't she?
6 Yale still loved her, didn't he?
7 Yale and Mary are back together again, aren't they ?
8 Yale is going to get a divorce, isn't he?
9 Ike is still on his own, isn't he?
10 The three are friends again now, aren't they?

Unit 9 Exercise 4

| 1 C | 3 F | 5 F | 7 C |
| 2 F | 4 C | 6 F | 8 F |

Unit 10 Exercise 1

a) 1 Is there a danger that genetic engineering might get out of control?
2 How do we know what may happen if we change genes?
3 What must I do if I need more information?
4 Who should take the responsibility for changing a person's genes?
5 Why should doctors tell us what to do?

Unit 10 Exercise 2

a) Suggested answers

1 What are the doctors' names?
2 What does the clinic do?
3 Who can use the clinic?
4 What is the success rate?
5 How many clinics are there in the US?
6 Who is Carmel Turner?
7 What did she say?

c) 2

Unit 10 Exercise 3

1 F	4 F	7 A	9 F
2 F	5 F	8 A	10 A
3 A	6 A		

Unit 10 Exercise 4

a) 1 break
2 bows
3 plane
4 threw
5 bread
6 some
7 Hi
8 groan
9 ate
10 attacks

Unit 11 Exercise 1

1 Although
2 on the one hand
3 on the other hand
4 Nevertheless/ However
5 while

Unit 11 Exercise 2

a) 1 'At' is used to show an exact point of time and with festivals.
2 'In' is used with years, seasons and months, with parts of the day, and to show a period when something will happen.
3 'By' indicates a limit to the time during which something will happen
4 'For' is used to show a period of time.
5 'Since' is used to show the start of a period in the past.
6 'On' is used with dates and days.

b) 1 at
2 in
3 at
4 By
5 In
6 On
7 for
8 at
9 since
10 in
11 at
12 for

Unit 11 Exercise 3

1 switchboard
2 reservations
3 check
4 double
5 bathrooms
6 booked
7 vacancies
8 rate
9 excluding
10 expiry

Unit 11 Exercise 4

b) 1 W   3 S   5 S   7 W
2 S   4 W   6 W   8 W

c) The strong form occurs when the preposition ends a sentence.

Unit 11 Exercise 5

1 b)   2 d)   3 c)   4 a)

Unit 12 Exercise 1

1 Why do the Japanese always smile
2 Why do they laugh
3 it is not funny
4 These questions are often asked
5 The Japanese laugh
6 they are amused
7 they are embarrassed
8 or are not sure
9 A common reason . . . is
10 A smile is used
11 The Japanese try
12 It does not mean
13 eye contact is seen
14 It is considered
15 whose status is higher
16 Japanese salesmen are taught
17 The fingers are used
18 They start
19 the fingers are folded
20 the fingers are opened
21 This way of counting is learnt

Unit 12 Exercise 2

1 blow
2 sneeze
3 rub
4 sneeze
5 covered
6 scratched
7 sucking
8 stroking
9 touched

Unit 12 Exercise 3

a) disagree, disappear, disbelieve, uncomfortable, unequal, dishonest, unkind, dislike (verb or noun)/unlike (adjective or preposition), disobey, dissatisfied/unsatisfied, distrust

b) workable, changeable, boyish, poorish, greenish, reasonable, respectable, fixable, doable, strongish, selfish, longish, blackish, shortish, thinkable, usable, teachable, amateurish, tigerish, believable, greyish, newish, oldish.

Unit 12 Exercise 4

b) 1 W   4 W   7 W   9 W
2 W   5 W   8 S   10 W
3 S   6 W

Unit 12 Exercise 5

1 c)   4 d)
2 e)   5 f)
3 b)   6 a)

Listening Practice 3

a) 1 and 2
b) 3

Unit 13 Exercise 1

a) 1 Name cards must be treated like the people themselves.
2 The name card should be presented with two hands and a bow.
3 The company card must be given first, then your own.
4 The card should be held so that it can be read (by the receiver).
5 A card must be looked at when it is given to you.
6 The cards will be printed in English and Japanese.
7 A meeting about the new factory is going to be held tomorrow.
8 Your meaning might be misunderstood.
9 Exactly what has to be done needs to be explained clearly.

b) 1 The engine must be turned off.
2 The windows must be closed.
3 The windscreen wipers should be fixed.
4 The coins should be inserted in the slot.
5 The programme required should be selected.
6 The car should be driven forward.
7 The brakes should be applied.
8 The engine should be started after the end of the wash.
9 The car should be driven out at once.

Unit 13 Exercise 2

a) 1 £18
2 Takeya
3 An overnight bus (£44.38)
4 Through adverts on Sundays in English language newspapers

b) 1 having
2 are used
3 out
4 on
5 taken
6 be understood
7 are taken
8 to agree
9 without
10 before
11 are asked
12 What
13 is held
14 accepted

Unit 13 Exercise 3

1 d)	4 i)	7 e)	10 g)
2 c)	5 f)	8 h)	11 a)
3 b)	6 k)	9 j)	

Unit 13 Exercise 4

1 a) pre'sent
2 b) ob'ject
3 a) im'ports
4 b) 'export
5 b) 'rejects

Unit 14 Exercise 1

1 Some houses have been rebuilt.
2 All electrical supplies have been restored.
3 Most people have been rehoused/compensated.
4 All roads have been reopened/rebuilt.
5 Some crops have been replanted.
6 Few rivers have been controlled.
7 Not all victims have been compensated/rehoused.
8 Most damage has been repaired.

Unit 14 Exercise 2

1 had been forecast	9 were flooded
2 was prepared	10 could not cope
3 came	11 broke
4 had been expected	12 were covered
5 fell	13 were washed
6 made	14 had been made
7 had been cleared	15 cannot be blamed
8 poured	16 should be praised

Unit 14 Exercise 3

1 journalists	4 cut, fit
2 read	5 fit
3 accuracy, clarity, presentation	

Unit 14 Exercise 4

Sun: drought, heat wave
Water: cloudburst, dew, downpour, drizzle, flood, fog, mist
Snow and ice: blizzard, frost, hail, sleet
Wind: breeze, gale, hurricane

Unit 14 Exercise 5

Al'gerian (S)	Vene'zuelan (S)
'Kenyan (S)	Aus'tralian (S)
Mo'roccan (S)	Indo'nesian (S)
Saudi A'rabian (S)	Ma'laysian (S)
South 'African (S)	Ko'rean (S)
'Syrian (S)	Is'raeli (D)
Tu'nisian (S)	Ku'waiti (S)
Argen'tinian (S)	Bangla'deshi (S)
Bo'livian (S)	Paki'stani (S)
Bra'zilian (S)	Leba'nese (D)
Ca'nadian (D)	Chi'nese (D)
'Chilean (S)	Japa'nese (D)
Co'lombian (S)	Nepa'lese (D)
'Cuban (S)	Taiwa'nese (D)
Ja'maican (S)	Vietna'mese (D)
'Mexican (S)	'Turkish (S)
Pe'ruvian (S)	'Thai (S)

Unit 14 Exercise 6

Suggested answers

1 'Pouring down' is an informal expression meaning raining very hard.
2 A person who isn't killed in an accident is a survivor.
3 Drizzle is a kind of fine rain. It's a bit like spray.
4 When you're soaking you are completely wet.
5 A victim is someone who is attacked or killed.
6 Something which is tragic is very sad.

Unit 15 Exercise 1

There are many possible answers here, depending on your own opinions. Here are some examples.

1 Computers will be used by everyone.
2 Typhoid will have been wiped out.
3 Holidays will have been made compulsory.
4 Cars will not be allowed in towns.
5 Marriage will have been abolished.
6 Children will be educated at home.
7 Work will have been made illegal.
8 Books will not have been replaced by computers.

Unit 15 Exercise 2

1 They believed that every person would be free. (W)
2 They thought that balloons would be the air transport of the future. (W)
3 They expected that there would be enough food for everyone. (W)
4 They were sure that women would not be given the vote. (W)
5 They thought that children would leave school at ten. (W)
6 They expected that there would be no more wars. (W)
7 They thought that French would be the world language. (W)
8 They thought that electric trains would be invented. (R)
9 They hoped that people would travel in space. (R)
10 They were sure that there would be political prisoners. (R)

Unit 15 Exercise 3

By 2020, having a room full of books will show you to be old-fashioned. Major works of reference will go first. No-one buys encyclopedias any more because it is far easier to search for information on a CD-Rom. But as screens become lighter and brighter and can have the thickness and size of a magazine, the electronic book will replace the novel. The advantages are that you can store hundreds of books, or download them from a terminal with a connection to the publisher. Instead of going to a bookshop, you'll be able to sample as many books as you like electronically, and take the whole book only if you want it.

Unit 15 Exercise 4

1 broken out
2 gone out
3 burst out
4 talk … over
5 put out
6 worn out
7 think … over
8 hand over

Unit 15 Exercise 5

1 rude
2 paid
3 said
4 dead
5 lead (go in front)
6 worse
7 divorce

Unit 16 Exercise 1

1 will have changed
2 will be working
3 will have developed
4 will have happened
5 will be learning
6 will have become
7 will they be doing
8 will be learning
9 will have been developed
10 will still be studying

Unit 16 Exercise 2

1 Will you be using the car tomorrow night?
2 Will you be going to the party on Saturday?
3 Will you be getting a birthday present for Sue?
4 Will you be wearing your red coat tomorrow?
5 Will you be going to the football match?

Unit 16 Exercise 4

1 by	16 see you
2 tend	17 I'll call
3 extremely	18 up
4 to	19 place
5 their	20 But
6 sure	21 not
7 never	22 seriously
8 with	23 mean
9 too	24 won't
10 in	25 again
11 with	26 Don't
12 If	27 telephone
13 like	28 Don't
14 always	29 up
15 with	30 place

Unit 16 Exercise 5

a)			
Arabic 1		Italian 7	
Chinese 5		Portuguese 8	
English 9		Japanese 2	
French 6		Spanish 4	
German 3			

b) 1 a)   2 d)   3 b)   4 c)

Listening Practice 4

a) false	g) true
b) true	h) true
c) false	i) true
d) true	j) true
e) false	k) false
f) true	l) false

TAPESCRIPTS

Unit 1 Exercise 4

1 Excuse me, what does this word mean?
2 Can you say that again, please?
3 I'm afraid I don't quite understand.
4 How do you spell that please?
5 Why do you say 'I like' and not 'I'm liking' ?
6 How do you pronounce this word please?
7 Excuse me, is this correct?
8 Is this how you spell 'engineer'?

Unit 3 Exercise 5

accepted	explained	picked
agreed	finished	prepared
asked	followed	reached
answered	gathered	recommended
attached	greeted	refused
bathed	happened	requested
believed	helped	retired
called	interviewed	showed
checked	invited	started
compared	joined	sunbathed
cooked	knocked	talked
corrected	listened	tested
declined	missed	tipped
described	needed	travelled
disappeared	noted	washed
discussed	noticed	wondered
dressed	opened	
expected	performed	

Unit 3 Exercise 6

1 full stop   2 comma   3 open brackets
4 close brackets   5 asterisk   6 equals   7 colon
8 semi-colon   9 open inverted commas
10 close inverted commas   11 exclamation mark
12 dash   13 plus   14 question mark   15 minus

Unit 4 Exercise 3(b)

A H J K
B C D E G P T V
F L M N S X Z
I Y
O
Q U W
R
Hello!
Two G and T . . .
Eh?
said, two G and T . . .
N.O.
Why?
see you two before . . .
Are you 18?
Oh hell!
Are 18!
Oh . . . you are, are you?
You see!
See!
Oh!
Oh . . . I see . . . 1978.
You too? . . . 18, are you?
Yes!
They are 18.
Are they? OK.
Two G and T?
Yes!
Here you are!
You see.

Unit 4 Exercise 4

1 Would you please be so kind as to shut up?
2 Would you mind if we turned the heating on?
3 Do you know if it's eleven o'clock yet?
4 Does everyone understand what they've got to do?
5 Would somebody mind closing the window?
6 Could you possibly finish now please?
7 Can anyone remember what we did in the last lesson?
8 Could you please remember to bring your dictionaries next time?
9 How about going over it again from the beginning, please?
10 Would you mind listening for a minute, please?

Listening Practice 1

Daniella: I can remember when I was young fighting with my brother. He was three years younger than me. He still is . . .
Ellia: He still is! Things didn't change?
Daniella: No, no.
Ellia: He still is. I like that.
Daniella: And . . . I can remember I tried to kill him once.
Aziz: Oh!
Daniella: Actually, I tried to kill him three times, but not all on purpose.
Ellia: Oh!
Daniella: The first . . . the first time was when he was a baby in his pram and I thought he looked a little bit cold, so I . . . I took all the cushions off the sofa and piled them on top of his face.
Ellia: Oh!
Daniella: I was . . . I was about three. My mother came and she said – I remember this so clearly – I remember she came into the room and she saw the pile of cushions on top of the pram . . .
Ellia: Yes?
Daniella: . . . 'My baby!', and she burst into tears and threw all the cushions off . . .
Ellia: Yes, yes?
Daniella: . . . all round the room and grabbed my brother and he was OK, and I remember she sat on the sofa and cried and cried and cried, and I didn't know why!
Ellia: What was going on . . . yes . . .
Daniella: Couldn't understand why! That was the first time. The second time was when I was a little bit older and I found a bottle of . . . children's aspirin . . .
Ellia: Ooooh!
Daniella: They were orange-flavoured and . . . I had a little cooker, a pretend cooker . . .
Ellia: Yes?
Daniella: . . . and I decided I was going to cook my brother some . . . a meal.
Ellia: With the aspirins?
Daniella: Yes, with my little plastic saucepans. So I got a plastic saucepan . . .
Ellia: Extremely naughty!
Daniella: . . . and I filled it with water. I know. And I put in all these orange tablets . . .
Ellia: Yes?
Daniella: . . . crushed them up and made like a soup.
Ellia: OK.
Daniella: And I said . . . I said to my brother, 'Here, I've made you some soup!' He was about two . . .
Ellia: Poor kid . . .
Daniella: And he drank the soup and of course he fell unconscious.
Ellia: He fell uncon . . .
Daniella: And . . . my mother found him and she phoned the doctor and the doctor – she was hysterical – she phoned the doctor and the doctor said, 'You've got to make him sick'. So, I have this picture of my little brother sitting in the kitchen on the . . . on the side, on the cabinet, and my father trying to pour salt water into his mouth – and he was, he was unconscious most of the time . . .
Ellia: Yes?
Daniella: . . . sticking his finger down his throat and my brother being sick everywhere. I remember watching this and my mother was sitting on the stairs sobbing, crying her eyes out, saying, 'Why did you do it?' and I really didn't understand what I'd done.
Ellia: You didn't know what . . . what you did?
Daniella: No. I just thought they were sweeties.
Ellia: Yes. Such a naughty girl!
Daniella: Yes. The third . . . the third time was . . .
Ellia: Is he alive?
Daniella: Yeah. That's why I said he was still three years younger! The third time I won't talk about. That was on purpose.
Ellia: Oh!
Daniella: It was just a very nasty fight we had . . .
Ellia: Hmm.
Daniella: When we were older.
Ellia: I see.

Unit 5 Exercise 5

1 I'm afraid I'm not quite sure what to do.
2 Do you mean that you want us to read the whole text?
3 I'm sorry, but we're not entirely sure what to do.
4 Could you please go over it again?
5 What you mean is that we've got to work in pairs.
6 Am I right in thinking that 'treasure' means something valuable?
7 What page did you want us to look at?
8 I don't understand why it's wrong.
9 Excuse me, but are we meant to do it on our own?
10 What do you want us to do after we've finished?

Unit 6 Exercise 5

1 I am afraid I don't understand.
2 Could you go over it again, please?
3 I'm afraid I didn't quite catch what you said.
4 Excuse me, how do you pronounce this word?
5 I'm having difficulty with this text.
6 Can you explain why this is wrong, please?
7 I don't understand what I've done wrong.
8 Why is this word pronounced like this?
9 I'm sorry, but I don't follow.
10 Excuse me, I don't know what to do.

Unit 8 Exercise 5

a) 'Marrying a man is like buying something you've been admiring for a long time in a shop window. You may love it when you get it home, but it doesn't always go with everything else in the house.'
b) 'Wives are people who feel they don't dance enough.'
c) 'I've only slept with the men I've been married to. How many women can make that claim?'
d) 'For a while we wondered whether to take a vacation or get a divorce. We decided that a trip to Bermuda is over in two weeks, but a divorce is something you always have.'
e) 'Take it from me – marriage isn't a word, it's a sentence.'
f) 'If you want to sacrifice the admiration of many men for the criticism of one, go ahead, get married.'
g) 'We would have broken up except for the children. Who were the children? Well, she and I were.'

Listening Practice 2

Charles: … but I feel terrible about it. What on earth can I do?

Presenter: Hmm. I'm sorry to hear that you're having so much trouble. Let's ask our psychiatrist to comment. Pamela?

Psychiatrist: Mmm. Hello. Yes, you do have a problem. The first bit of advice I want to give you is: you shouldn't feel guilty about feeling angry, upset or not liking her. This is quite natural under the circumstances. Now, have you tried to talk to her about this?

Charles: Oh, yes, several times. But, it's no good – she just doesn't care. Sometimes she apologises, but she doesn't change.

Psychiatrist: Mmm, this aggression is very worrying. We can, of course, expect some aggression at times. Indeed, this is quite normal as they try to come to terms with the changes in their bodies and their lives. However, I think you should call the police next time she hits you or threatens you or anyone else. It might be just the shock she needs.

Charles: Yeah, yeah maybe.

Psychiatrist: She needs to know she can't just do these things.

Charles: I suppose so, but …

Counsellor: May I just come in here?

Presenter: Yes, David.

Counsellor: As a community counsellor I see similar problems quite often. You're not alone, by any means. Often it's, it's a matter of trust. Tell me, do you trust … what's her name?

Charles: Emma. No, not at all. Not any more.

Counsellor: Mmm. Do you find yourself nagging her all the time?

Charles: Er, yeah. About homework, definitely. Of course. She'd never do it if I didn't! She's so lazy in the house! I mean, it's unacceptable.

Counsellor: Mmm, well, I think, if I were you, I'd stop. Tell her that if she can think of something useful she wants to do with her life, you would be happy to help her try it, but that you won't support her if she is lazy or abusive or violent. If she wants to be like this, she must leave home.

Charles: Throw her out, you mean? How could I do that? She's only …

Counsellor: I think you should say that, yes. She has to learn to take the consequences of her actions. It might be a good idea to suggest to her that she finds a flat with some friends and gets a job to pay the rent. Let her see that you think she is old enough and mature enough to do this.

Charles: You're kidding!

Counsellor: No. No. You see, my guess is she won't want to leave home.

Presenter: I'm sorry, we have to finish there. We have another caller. I hope our experts have given you some good advice. Goodbye … and good luck! And now, our next caller …

Peter: … well, it's so hard to talk about it, you know.

Presenter: Yes, Peter, we can understand that, but please don't worry. Our panel of experts are here to give you advice and help you. Let's ask Pamela, our psychiatrist. Why do you think she acts this way and what can Peter do about it?

Psychiatrist: Mmm. Actually, it's not that uncommon a problem these days. It's just that people, especially men, don't like to talk about it. That's perfectly understandable, of course.

Presenter: Mmm.

Psychiatrist: Well, we need to find out more about … what's her name, Peter?

Peter: Janice.

Psychiatrist: Janice. Do you know anything about her childhood?

Peter: Well, her parents were very strict – her father, in particular. She hates him and doesn't speak to him any more. Hasn't seen him for years. Her mother's dead.

Psychiatrist: I see. Hmm. Tell me, what sort of things does she do and what seems to trigger her attacks?

Peter: Well, sometimes it's alcohol, I think. Last Saturday, for instance, we'd been out to the pub and had a few drinks with some friends. She was in a really good mood, you know? We got back home and we settled down to watch Match of the Day on the TV before going to bed.

Psychiatrist: She likes football, does she?

Peter: Well, it's me really who likes it … but, anyway, she went into the kitchen to make a cup of coffee and … well, I was just sitting there, like, watching the TV, when she threw a cup of hot coffee all over me and then attacked me with a knife.

Psychiatrist: Knife? Oh!

Peter: Yeah, a big bread knife. It caught me on my hand as I tried to cover my face. I had blood everywhere. She was like a wild thing, kicking and punching me. Luckily, I'm bigger than her and eventually she stopped, and then ran upstairs and locked herself in the bedroom. I drove to the hospital and had my hand stitched. I said I'd cut myself.

Psychiatrist: How terrible for you. How often does it happen?

Peter: Oh, about twice a month.

Psychiatrist: Mmm. Oh dear. And what do you do?

Peter: Well, if I try to hit back, she just gets worse. I usually try to hold her down or I go out of the house.

Psychiatrist: Mmm. Well, it's clear that she needs some psychiatric assessment and probably the best way to approach this is to talk to your doctor.

Presenter: Doctor, do you agree?

Doctor: Yes, yes, I do. It seems Janice may need a referral, perhaps to a hospital, and you both need a good deal of counselling, I'd say.

Peter: Yes. It's just so … so difficult to talk about it. I feel so stupid … a grown man …

Doctor: You have to put these feelings aside. Getting Janice well again must be your first priority.

Peter: Yes, I suppose so.

Doctor: You know, if I were you, I'd contact the local council and find out about support groups for battered husbands. They do exist you know.

Peter: Really? I thought …

Doctor: You thought you were the only one? No no. No, you're not. I think, too, it'd be a good idea for you to have the chance to discuss these problems with other men in similar situations.

Peter: OK, right. Yeah. Thank you.

Presenter: Well, Peter, we hope we've been of some help. Good luck. And now it's time to finish for today. Thank you to all our callers for allowing us to share their problems. Our experts today were Pamela …

Unit 9 Exercise 1

Ike: I don't understand what's happening any more. It's like my whole life is falling apart. First you told me that Mary found me attractive.

Yale: Yes, that's what she told me.

Ike: So I asked her to marry me.

Yale: And?

Ike: She told me that she wouldn't marry me yet. I asked her what she thought of me and she told me that she thought of me as the father of her child! I was so happy I nearly jumped out of the window!

Yale: And?

Ike: Then yesterday she told me that she still loved you. I was shocked. I didn't know what to say.

Yale: What did you say?

Ike: I called her a liar. I called her a cheat and a liar.

Yale: Oh no.

Ike: Yeah. It was a mistake. She called me so many names back I can't remember them all, and maybe some weren't English anyway, and then she left.

Yale: Did she tell you where she was going?

Ike: Yeah. To your apartment. Oh, if you see her, can you ask her for my key back, please, and my clarinet.

Unit 9 Exercise 3

Ike's really silly, isn't he?

1. You've heard the latest about Ike, haven't you?
2. He's living with Mary, isn't he?
3. She and Yale were friends, weren't they?
4. Ike and Mary used to argue, didn't they?
5. Mary left Ike, didn't she?
6. Yale still loved her, didn't he?
7. Yale and Mary are back together again, aren't they?
8. Yale is going to get a divorce, isn't he?
9. Ike is still on his own, isn't he?
10. The three are friends again now, aren't they?

Unit 11 Exercise 5

1. Do you mind if I leave ten minutes early?
2. Is it all right if we don't complete all of it?
3. Can I open a window, please?
4. We'd like to finish now. Is that OK?

Unit 12 Exercise 5

1. Excuse me, I didn't say 'bed' I said 'bid'.
2. I beg your pardon, I thought you wanted us to start.
3. I'm terribly sorry, but isn't it time to finish now?
4. I may be wrong, but isn't the answer 'yes'?
5. I'm probably wrong about this, I thought you said page 30.
6. Excuse me, there's a bit of a problem. We don't know what to do.

Listening Practice 3

Teresa: What is it we're supposed to do now? Did you … did you …

Eric: Oh blimey … group work.

Teresa: Oh, discuss in groups …?

Pam: Yeah, discuss what we think harassment is.

Gordon: … actually means, right?

Eric: Oh I don't. know. What a waste of time. I've got so much to do.

Pam: Oh look, we all have.

Teresa: Yeah, shut up, Eric.

Pam: Right, now, what do we think harassment is? Um … Anyone experienced any?

Eric: Oh crumbs … what a waste of time …

Gordon: I … I have. I had an experience recently.

Pam: OK.

Teresa: Experience of harassment?

Gordon: Yeah.

Eric: Right! Oh yeah!

Pam: Go on, Gordon.

Gordon: Well … maybe … I don't know, maybe it's a bit silly.

Teresa: No no, we all want to know.

Eric: Get on with it Gordon.

Gordon: Well, I think we get bullied at work.

Pam: Bullied, yeah, that's a good way of putting it!

Gordon: Yeah, I mean, not mentioning any names or anything, but haven't you been pressurised into doing things at work you felt were wrong, or threatened if you objected to anything?

Teresa: Well, I know who you're referring to!

Pam: Oh yes, yes. Dale Grunt, our beloved director.

Gordon: Yeah well, anyway, I think the way he stops you in the corridor is harassment.

Eric: Oh yeah, I know what you mean.

Gordon: Like, last week, he stopped me outside the men's toilet, when he could see I was in a hurry. 'Oh Gordon,' he says, 'I notice your figures are down again this month. Er … when is it your contract finishes?' Yeah. Before I could say much, he walked off. I got left feeling really humiliated.

Eric: Yeah, it makes you feel really insecure, doesn't it?

Gordon: Yeah, exactly.

Pam: Threatened, I'd say!

Teresa: Mmm, intimidated! Yes, and you know what he did to me last week?

Pam: Tell us!

Teresa: I got this phone call from his secretary. He wanted to see me straight away in his office.

Pam: What about?

Teresa: Well, that's just it, I didn't know! I worried all the way there and felt really nervous when I got there. I just knew it was something bad. I kept thinking, 'Oh Lord, what have I done, what have I done?' Remember that time he told me off at a committee meeting for making an error in that … that costing?

Pam: Ay, right, I remember. Ooh I did feel for you! That was just outrageous, in front of all those people!

Gordon: But he does that all the time! He did it to me at that meeting. . .

Eric: Go on, Teresa.

Gordon: Oh yeah, sorry. Carry on, yeah.

Teresa: Well, I wondered if I'd got it wrong again, you know. But I couldn't think! But I felt guilty anyway.

Eric: What was it about, then?

Teresa: Ha! Well, what do you think – he only wanted me to take on Dorothy's work while she's away on holiday.
Pam: Bloody cheek! You're not his secretary!
Teresa: I know, but . . .
Eric: Well, I hope you told him no!
Teresa: That's just it . . . I, er . . . well, I was . . . so relieved it wasn't anything bad, I said yes.
Pam: Oh no!
Teresa: I felt so stupid! I was so angry!
Eric: Well, you mustn't let him get away with stuff like that!
Teresa: Yeah, well, it's easy for you to say that, isn't it? You're not on a temporary contract!
Gordon: Yeah, that's right. It's different then. You feel very vulnerable. You can't stand up to him because you have to think of the next contract.
Pam: So I suppose we've all experienced his little ways of manipulating us, haven't we?
Eric: Yeah, well he tried it on me not long ago. Stopped me in the corridor and said, 'Eric, I've been thinking about your request for more administrative staff. You know, if you were to get that Malaysian contract, it would give you a good basis for employing another secretary for your department. Think about it.' Then he walked off. I mean he knows damn well that the Malaysian contract would mean so much extra work we'd need several new people, not one. We need one now, but the implied threat was, 'If you don't get that contract, I won't allow you to have the help you need.'
Gordon: Typical!
Eric: Oh, I know his game. He wanted that contract because it would add to the export figures and make him look good and if he could do it without increasing staffing costs too much, he'd look even better.
Pam: So what did you do?
Eric: Well, I followed him into the men's toilet and said, 'About that Malaysian contract – nice try, mate!' and then I slapped him on the back and laughed. Made a joke of it!
Pam: Blimey, whatever did he do?
Eric: Well, he was busy, if you know what I mean, so I walked out before he could say anything. Gave him a taste of his own medicine. I felt great!
Gordon: Wow, good for you! But you can get away with things like that, being on a permanent contract, can't you?
Teresa: And you're a man. And a head of department.
Pam: Well that's right.
Teresa: Anyway, I wonder if you have got away with it, Eric? I mean, has he got you more staff?
Eric: Er . . . well, no, I haven't heard anything yet.
Pam: No, I thought not. You know what he said to me last month? You won't believe it!
Eric: God, he's a prat!
Pam: What he said was . . .
Eric: I'd like to kick him down the stairs!
Pam: What he said was . . . Well, when I told him I thought I was overworked he said, 'Well, Pam, perhaps you'd be happier at a lower grade in another department.'
Teresa: No! You're kidding!
Pam: He did, he did. I tell you, he did. Can you imagine?
Gordon: That's despicable.
Teresa: You know, I'm not sure. I mean, do you think it really is harassment? Maybe it's just management style. Don't you think? Do you think he knows he's doing it?
Eric: Some management style! I mean, of course he does. Divide and rule!
Gordon: Management style? Well, I think . . .
Pam: No, I don't think his ways of doing things are right. I mean, it doesn't help the team spirit, does it? If he makes us feel . . . well, what? . . . pressurised, inadequate, insecure, well I call that harassment.
Gordon: I think that . . .
Eric: Yeah, absolutely. I agree.
Gordon: I think that he does it all on purpose.
Pam: Yes.
Gordon: Some days I can't bear the thought of coming into work. Have you heard how he talks to Dorothy sometimes? It's appalling. I wonder she doesn't walk out.
Pam: Well, she needs the job, just like we all do.
Teresa: Mmm, that's right.
Pam: So er . . . So, can . . . can we agree then that harassment is behaviour that makes you feel small, worthless, insecure . . .
Teresa: Threatened . . . bullied . . .
Pam: Yeah, that if someone's behaviour makes you feel all those things then you are being harassed?

Eric: Hmm, some people might feel they're being bullied, but you know, others may not. It depends on your personality and how you feel.
Teresa: And what your status is.
Gordon: Well, I think the thing is that if you *feel* you are being harassed or bullied, then you probably are. If you feel ill at the thought of coming to work, then . . .
Teresa: It's very tricky, isn't it?
Gordon: But, but we all feel we *are* being bullied by our boss, right? We all think he should stop behaving like that, right? That his behaviour is not appropriate?
Eric: Yeah, yeah, right. Come on, let's write that on the flipchart, anyway. Pam, you can do that, can't you?
Pam: What!
Others: Oh! Oh Eric!

Unit 13 Exercise 2(a)

Imagine the expression on the face of the new visitor who has just flown into Tokyo and been foolish enough to get a taxi from the airport to the centre of Tokyo. The fare is £200 and possibly more if the traffic is bad! Trying to forget the pain of giving the taxi driver so much money, the visitor goes to a restaurant near the hotel, eager to taste the famous raw fish. But the cheapest dinner is £50! The visitor goes back to the hotel and orders a beer – only to find that it costs £10!

But Japan needn't cost as much as this. Knowing what to do is the secret. For example, getting from Narita Airport to Tokyo costs only £5.85 on a slow train and £18 on an express train – a lot less than £200! You can also find reasonably priced restaurants and hot noodles can always be found near any railway station for £3.75 for a bowl. The Takeya restaurant, that's T-A-K-E-Y-A, offers all the grilled beef you can eat for £11.25 for women and £12.50 for men.

Want a cheap way of getting to China? Forget the overpriced airfares – take the ferry from Yokohama to Shanghai. At £156 one-way, it's half the price of the plane. Similarly, overnight buses to Kyoto at £44.38 are about half the price of the bullet train ticket. A Japan rail pass can save huge amounts on the railways but it must be bought outside Japan at a Japan Tourism Office or Japan Airlines office.

If you really want to buy a kimono as a souvenir or present, watch out for special sales of used wedding kimonos at department stores. They're often reduced from the new price of more than £6000 to as little as £62.50. And if you've got nowhere to stay and it is late at night, try one of the 'love hotels' – these are intended for couples to use for short stays and often have vacancies after 11 pm for as little as £37 for the night – as long as you don't mind the mirror in the ceiling!

There are lots of useful guidebooks including *Living for Less in Tokyo – and Liking it!*, *Japan – a Budget Travel Guide* and *Japan, Cheap and Easy* which has good advice for anyone coming to live in Japan. It tells you where you can rent useful things and also suggests buying cheap furniture and things for the home from foreigners who are leaving. You can find them through adverts on Sundays in English-language newspapers. Finally, a very useful guide to food is *Eating Cheap in Japan* which includes such information as the ingredients of 43 different noodle dishes.

Unit 13 Exercise 2(b)

Foreigners usually misunderstand the way business or office meetings work in Japan. In fact, when they work well, the Japanese way of having meetings is really good – and far better than what we are used to in the West. I lived in Japan for a couple of years and at the start I couldn't work out what was happening at meetings – they used to go on for hours and hours but no decisions were taken. The first thing that has to be understood is that decisions are not taken at Japanese meetings. The decisions are taken before the meeting, and the purpose of the meeting is for everyone to agree to the decision. Of course, decisions aren't taken without asking people what they think, but this happens before the meeting. You are asked your opinion and can express your views before the meeting takes place. What you say is considered carefully and a decision is taken. Then a meeting is held and the decision is accepted by everyone – the decision is now something which everyone 'owns'.

Unit 14 Exercise 3

The journalists type their stories straight into the system and then they're sent to the newsdesk, which is this area, where they're read and assessed for their news value. The chief sub-editor reads and assesses them for their news value and decides which page and where they're going to go, and then they come to the subs. Well, the sub-editor's job is really concerned with three things: accuracy, clarity and presentation. After we've subbed (er, sub-edited) our stories and they've been placed on the page, which again we do electronically these days, it's all done on computer – when all the stories fit that space – because we've got the other element of the sub's job, which is to cut the stories to fit, because often they're way over length – the page is typeset as a whole page.

Unit 14 Exercise 5

Algerian	Chilean
Kenyan	Colombian
Moroccan	Cuban
Saudi Arabian	Jamaican
South African	Mexican
Syrian	Peruvian
Tunisian	Venezuelan
Argentinian	Australian
Bolivian	Indonesian
Brazilian	Malaysian
Canadian	Korean
Israeli	Bangladeshi
Kuwaiti	Pakistani
Lebanese	Nepalese
Chinese	Taiwanese
Japanese	Vietnamese
Turkish	Thai

Unit 16 Exercise 4

Cariocas, by nature, tend to be extremely open, warm and friendly. And to show their friendliness, you can be sure that they never say farewell with a simple 'goodbye'. It would be just too dry and not in keeping with their nature. If you want to behave like a real Carioca, always end a conversation with one of the following:

"A gente se ve": See you!
"Te ligo": I'll call you.
"Aparece em casa": Show up at my place at any time.

But remember! These phrases are not to be taken seriously. In other words they mean:

"We won't be seeing each other again soon."
"Don't wait for my telephone call."
"Don't show up at my place."

Listening Practice 4

Interviewer: And now let's turn to the prospect of life in the future. One family believes firmly that a new life is waiting for them sometime in the future. They are the Blackmans and when they die, Paula and her husband, Bob, and their son, Max, will be frozen until scientific advances allow them to be brought back to life. Should that happen, their daughter, Emily, will not be with them. Now, the Blackmans are currently the only family in Britain prepared to be frozen so that they can be rejuvenated and revived in the future and they've been much in the news recently. Let's talk to them and find out why they're doing this and why Emily has refused their invitation to immortality. First of all, Bob Blackman, was it your idea to freeze your family?
Bob: Well, yes, I suppose it was. We'd been discussing it for some time, though.
Interviewer: Did you agree straight away, Paula, or did you need persuading?
Paula: Well, like Bob said, we'd been discussing it on and off for years and then we saw an advertisement for a cryogenics unit in Michigan and decided to get more details.

Interviewer: But why do you want to do this? Is it an interest in life in the future – a kind of time travelling adventure – or are you just afraid to die?

Bob: I'm not interested in travelling through time: there isn't a year I would particularly like to be brought back in. I just want to be alive again as soon as possible.

Interviewer: But, surely, if you die as an old man, you'll be revived as an old man? I mean, why bother?

Bob: No, no. I often get asked this. You see, what people don't understand is that by the time it's possible to reactivate a body, it'll also be possible to rejuvenate it, as well.

Interviewer: Ah, so you'd wake up younger?

Bob: That's right. And healthier.

Interviewer: Right. So what age would you like to be?

Bob: Oh, I'll be like I was when I was 23 or 24, when everything was at optimum levels, at my peak, as it were.

Interviewer: Hmm. Paula, don't you think your family is, well, how shall I put it, rather obsessed with death?

Pam: Not at all, not at all.

Bob: No, no.

Pam: We want to live!

Interviewer: Would you do anything differently the second time around?

Pam: Would I do anything differently? Um . . . well, I don't think I want to have children next time. It's not just that you have a family already, but there's a lot involved. I mean, you don't know until you've done it and then you have to get on with it. I was 19 when I started my family, which is young. If I had known how hard it was going to be, I wouldn't have done it.

Interviewer: So you see this as your second chance, an opportunity to deal with any regrets you have about this present life?

Pam: Yes, that's a good way of putting it, I suppose.

Interviewer: Right. Now, Max, you're 15 now. How do you feel about being frozen when you die?

Max: Well, when dad suggested it I was only 11, so it sounded really interesting. I mean, the process is . . . first, they get all your blood out and replace it with a special chemical, a type of anti-freeze, I think, and then you get put in a metal container full of liquid nitrogen and, oh yes, you're put in upside down so that, so that if there's a leak, your . . . your head gets affected last, you know? and might be saved. And anyway, then you're shipped to Michigan and . . . stored.

Interviewer: Oh! Sounds gruesome!

Max: Yeah! Wicked!

Interviewer: How do you feel about it? What do you think it'll be like to wake up in the future?

Max: I don't know, really. I suppose the only bad thing might be the way people react when you come back in the future. They might treat you like a rat in a laboratory because you're something different. The most exciting thing about it is the thought of coming back and seeing what the future's like – the music and that. I think the only thing I will really miss is Biohazard, my favourite heavy-metal band.

Interviewer: How do you feel about your sister not being there with you?

Max: Well, I didn't care when I was 11. I hated her. Now we get on better, but I think, really, it's her decision, isn't it? I wouldn't try to change her mind.

Interviewer: Emily, why don't you want to join your family in their new life in the future?

Emily: Well, well I don't think I could handle it, you know, if it did work. It could take millions of years and you wouldn't know when you were coming back or what you were coming back to. Everything will be so different. You won't have any of your things from home or the people who were part of your life before – only your family, and then . . . and then you'll be stuck with them forever. And suppose you get treated like some kind of alien? I don't want to come back and be treated like some kind of freak. If you remember your past life, you'll be like some . . . some walking history book. If you didn't, you wouldn't even know if you'd been married or had a child.

Bob: Well, it might not be like that. Personally, I think that by the year 2007 they'll be able to freeze a monkey and revive it three months later. Within 150 years they'll be able to do it to humans.

Emily: Oh, I'm not convinced. And another problem I've been thinking about is, is like, what happens when you and mum die? Do I mourn? Do I think, 'Oh never mind, they're not really dead. They'll come back in the future'? I think that will be really hard, you know.

Interviewer: You mean that you wouldn't know how to cope with the grieving process?

Emily: Yes. And anyway, I think . . . I think that even when you die . . . when you die, you know, your spirit or whatever leaves your body. All that will be frozen is just a lump of meat. Where will your spirit be when they revive you? I can't get my head around that!

Interviewer: Hmm. Bob, how do you feel about this?

Bob: Well, obviously, I think it's worth doing, but I respect Emily's decision and I won't try to change her mind.

Interviewer: Well, our listeners have heard your feelings on the matter, they've heard a little about the processes involved, but what does it cost to be immortalised in this way?

Bob: Oh, you're talking about roughly £23,000 per person. For the prospect of immortality, I think that's a pretty low price.

Interviewer: Well, thank you to the Blackman family for sharing their thoughts on immortality with us. Any regrets about your decisions?

Bob: No, not at all.

Paula: Of course not.

ACKNOWLEDGEMENTS

The authors and publishers are grateful to the following copyright owners for permission to reproduce copyright material. Every endeavour has been made to contact copyright owners and apologies are expressed for any omissions.

p. 6: Bradt Publications for text adapted from *Guide to Madagascar* by Hilary Bradt; p. 10: Thames & Hudson for the extract from *David Hockney by David Hockney. The Early Years*; p. 13: Posy Simmonds for the *ABC* cartoon; p. 16: ACTIONAID for text adapted from *Families: is there a fitting image?* by Jane Watterson; p. 18: 'The Astronaut' from *Little Johnny's Confessions* by Brian Patten, published by George Allen & Unwin, an imprint of HarperCollins *Publishers* Ltd; p. 18: 'Hair today, no her tomorrow' from *Storm Damage* by Brian Patten, © Brian Patten, 1988, reproduced by permission of the author c/o Rogers, Coleridge & White Ltd., 20 Powis Mews, London, W11 1JN; p. 21: IPC Magazines for adapted text from *Living* magazine; p. 23: Aurum Press Ltd and Little, Brown and Company for quotes from *The Book of Lists: The 90's Edition* by David Wallechinsky. Copyright © 1993 David Wallechinsky and Amy Wallace, published in the UK at £9.99 by Aurum Press Ltd, 1994, and in the US by Little, Brown and Company; p. 25: Virago Press and Deborah Tannen for text adapted from *That's Not What I Meant* by Deborah Tannen; p. 29: The Independent for 'Youth Survey', adapted from *Girls stick with traditional view of jobs for the boys* by Peter Wilby, © The Independent; p. 31: Times Publishing Group for 'Non-verbal communication in Japan' adapted from *Culture Shock! Japan* by Rex Shelley, © Times Books International; p. 34 & tapescripts on p. 49: The Independent for texts adapted from *Out of Japan* by Terry McCarthy, © The Independent; p. 39: IPC Magazines for 'Close the book!' from *Tales of the Unexpected* by A. Anderson in the New Scientist; p. 41: Priscilla Ann Goslin for text adapted from *How To Be A Carioca*.

The author and publishers are grateful to the following illustrators and photographic sources:

Illustrators: Ian Dicks: pp. 10, 28, 35; Steve Gyapay: p. 6; Phil Healey: pp. 19, 36; John Ireland: p. 31; Stephen May: pp. 8, 14, 15, 39, 40; Ron Mercer: pp. 9, 27; Jill Newton: p. 38; Meilo So: pp. 17, 22, 37; Kath Walker: p. 20.

Photographic sources: *David Hockney. Self Portrait, 1954* © Artists Collection / Bridgeman Art Library, London: p. 10; Barnabys Picture Library: p. 23 *m* & *r*; Camera Press Ltd / Karsh of Ottawa: p. 12 *r*; Camera Press Ltd / Iain McKell: p. 18; J Allan Cash Photolibrary: p. 34; Maggie Murray / Format Partners Photo Library: p. 31; Hulton Getty: p. 12 *l*; John R. Jones: p. 6; Louvre, Paris / Bridgeman Art Library, London: p. 23 *l*.
All other photographs taken by Steve Bond at F64.

l = left   *r* = right   *m* = middle

Picture research by Sandie Huskinson-Rolfe of PHOTOSEEKERS.

Copyright research and clearance by Sophie Dukan.

Edited by Meredith Levy.

Design by QuintonWong.

WORDLIST

Dieses Wörterverzeichnis enthält in alphabetischer Reihenfolge Wörter und Redewendungen aus den Units 1 bis 16 sowie dem Listening Practice 1 bis 4. Der Wortschatz des Waystage-Level und des Lehrwerks Activate Your English, Pre-intermediate wurde nicht in diese Liste aufgenommen.

Unregelmäßige Verben sind mit * gekennzeichnet. Hinter der deutschen Bedeutung finden Sie die Fundstelle des jeweiligen Stichworts, z. B. 6/2 = Unit 6 Übung 2, oder LP 2 = Listening Practice 2, 3 Ts/6 = Unit 3, Tapescript 6. Kursive Einträge kennzeichnen Wörter in den Hörtexten. Stichwörter, die nicht am Anfang einer Wendung stehen, sind unterstrichen.

A

abolish	abschaffen 15/1
abusive	beleidigend LP 2
accidentally	zufällig, versehentlich 7/3
accommodation	Unterkunft, Hotelzimmer 11/3
according to	je nach, entsprechend LP 1/1
account for	stellen, ausmachen 11/1
acquaintance	Bekanntschaft 16/5
action plan	Vorgehensweise 7/3
actually	*um genau zu sein, eigentlich, tatsächlich LP1*
administrative staff	*Verwaltungsangestellte (Plural) LP 3*
admiration	Bewunderung 8/5
advertisement	Anzeige, Reklame 2/1
advice	Rat, Ratschlag 1/1
give* advice	Ratschläge erteilen 1/1
alien	*Außerirdische/r LP 4*
all-out	bedingungslos, total 15/4
although	obwohl 2/1
appalling	*entsetzlich LP 3*
apply for	sich bewerben um 2/2
apply the brakes	bremsen, Bremse treten/ anziehen 13/1
approximate	ungefähr 11/2
argue	streiten 5/1
armed forces	Armee 11/1
as it were	*sozusagen LP 4*
assess	auswerten 14 Ts/3
psychiatric assessment	*psychiatrisches Gutachten LP 2*
asterisk	Sternchen 3 Ts/6
authorities	Behörden 14/2
availability	Verfügbarkeit 11/3
average	Durchschnitt, durchschnittlich 2/3
avoid	vermeiden 1/1
avoidance	Vermeidung 12/1

B

barbaric	unmenschlich, barbarisch 10/4
basics	Grundlagen 2 Ts/3
battered husbands	*geschlagene Ehemänner LP 2*
be pressurised into doing*	*gedrängt werden, etwas zu tun LP 3*
beloved	*geliebte/r LP 3*
betrayal of trust	Vertrauensbruch 7/3
bleat	blöken 5/3
bleed*	bluten 3/4
Blimey!	*Verflucht! LP 3*
blizzard	Schneesturm 14/4
bloke	„Kerl", Mann 5/2
Bloody cheek!	*Was für eine Unverschämtheit! LP 3*
booking office	Vorverkaufsstelle 11/3
bottom	unterhalb 3/7
bough	Ast 10/4
bow	Bug 10/4
brackets	Klammern 3 Ts/6
break	Pause 2 Ts/3
break* up	sich trennen 8/5
breed*	aufziehen, züchten 10/4
breeze	Brise 14/4
British Medical Association	britische Ärztevereinigung 10/2
bullet train	Bezeichnung für den japanischen Hochgeschwindigkeitszug „Shinkansen" 13 Ts/2a
bully	drangsalieren, unter Druck setzen LP 3
bully	jemand, der andere drangsaliert LP 3
burglar	Einbrecher 1/2
business executive	Manager 1/2

C

capable of	fähig sein, etw. zu tun 4/2
she doesn't <u>care</u>	*es ist ihr egal LP 2*
caress	streicheln 1/1
catch*	fangen, verstehen 3/4
catch* a cold	einen Schnupfen bekommen, sich erkälten 5/1
challenge	Herausforderung 12/1
chase out of	verjagen, wegjagen 4/2
cheat	Betrüger/in 9/1
Cheerio!	Tschüß! 16/6
Cheers!	Tschüß! Danke! Prost! 16/6
make* a <u>claim</u>	etwas behaupten 8/5
colon	Doppelpunkt 3 Ts/6
come as a surprise	überraschen, verblüffen 9/2
comedian	Komödiant/in 2/2
May I just <u>come</u> in here?	*Darf ich hier einhaken? LP 2*
commence	beginnen, anfangen 3/1
committee meeting	*Ausschußsitzung LP 3*
common	gebräuchlich 12/3
community counsellor	Gemeindeberater/in LP 2
compensate	eine Entschädigung erhalten 14/1
make* <u>compulsory</u>	verpflichtend machen 15/1
computer operator	Operator, jemand, der eine Großrechenanlage bedient 1/2
conclusion	Schlußfolgerung 9/5
confession	Beichte 6/1
confined to	beschränkt auf 4/2
conjunction	Konjunktion, Bindewort 2/4
consider carefully	sorgfältig bedenken 13/2
consumer goods	Verbrauchsgüter 10/3
contract	*Vertrag LP 3*
get* out of <u>control</u>	außer Kontrolle geraten 10/1
convenience	öffentliche Toilette, Bedürfnisanstalt 11/3
cope	aufnehmen, fertigwerden mit 14/2
costing	*Kalkulation LP 3*
counting	Zählen 12/1
That just about <u>covers</u> everything.	Das wär's dann wohl. 9/4
crop	Feldfrucht, Ernte 14/1
Crumbs!	*Mensch! LP 3*
crush something up	*etwas zerstoßen LP 1*
cryonic	tiefgekühlt LP 4
cushion	Kissen LP 1/2
customary	üblich 1/1
it is <u>customary</u>	es ist Brauch 1/1

D

dash	Gedankenstrich 3 Ts/6
deal* with	sich kümmern um 8/1

Dear me!	*Ach du meine Güte! Ach du liebe Zeit! LP 1*
decay	verfallen 6/1
decline	ablehnen, niedergehen, untergehen 3/5
definite article	bestimmter Artikel 2/4
depend on	abhängen von 1/1
despicable	*abscheulich LP 3*
devastated	völlig am Ende LP 2
dew	Tau 14/4
disloyalty	Untreue 7/3
doll	Puppe LP 1/2
dominate	dominieren 11/1
double	Doppelzimmer 11/3
doubt	Zweifel 6/3
download	installieren, laden 15/3
downpour	Platzregen, Wolkenbruch 14/2
dress	sich anziehen 3/5
drizzle	Nieselregen 14/4
drought	Dürre 14/4
dust	Staub 12/2
dusty	staubig 12/2

E

eager to do something	sich darauf freuen, etwas zu tun 13 Ts/2a
efficient	gut, effizient 9/2
embarrass	verlegen machen 12/1
embarrassment	Verlegenheit 7/3
enable	in die Lage versetzen 16/1
engine	Motor 13/1
enquire	sich erkundigen nach 11/3
environmental damage	Umweltschäden 9/5
equals	ist gleich (=) 3 Ts/6
escape	entkommen 8/1
especially	besonders 2 Ts/3
exactly	genau 13/1
examination results	Prüfungsergebnisse 4/1
exceed	überschreiten 11/3
exception	Ausnahme 2 Ts/3
exclamation mark	Ausrufezeichen 3 Ts/6
expense	Kosten 11/3
expiry date	Ablauftermin 11/3
extended family	Großfamilie 5/2

F

factory	Fabrik 4/1
fall* apart	aus den Fugen geraten 9/1
fare	Fahrgeld, Fahrkosten 13 Ts/2a
she was <u>fast</u> asleep	sie schlief fest 5/3
I did <u>feel</u> *for you!*	*Du tatest mir echt leid! LP 3*
ferry	Fähre 13 Ts/2a
festivals	Feiertage, Festspiele 11/2
fight	*Streit, Prügelei LP 1*
the global <u>figure</u>	die weltweite Zahl 5/2

fire brigade	Feuerwehr 11/1
flipchart	*Flipchart LP 3*
flood disaster	Überschwemmungs-katastrophe 14/2
focus on	sich konzentrieren auf LP 1/2
foolish	dumm 13 Ts/2a
for hours and hours	stundenlang 13/2
foreign	ausländisch 2/1
fraternal	brüderlich 5/2
full stop	Punkt 3 Ts/6

G

gale	Sturm 14/4
general population	Gesamtbevölkerung 4/2
gerund	Gerundium 2/4
get* away with something	*sich etwas erlauben können LP 3*
get* benefit	profitieren von … 1/5
get* on with	*weitermachen mit LP 3*
giggle	kichern 12/1
global	weltweit 5/2
go* with	passen zu 8/5
govern	bestimmen 1/1
graduate	(Hochschul-)Absolvent/in, Schulabgänger/in 2/2
grieving process	*Trauerarbeit LP 4*
groan	Stöhnen 10/4
grow*	wachsen, anbauen 10/4
gruesome	grausig, schauerlich LP 4
guilty	*schuldig LP 2*

H

habit	Gewohnheit 1/5
get* into the habit of	sich angewöhnen 1/5
hail	Hagel 14/4
happy-go-lucky	unbekümmert, sorglos 7/3
harassment	Schikanieren, Belästigung LP 3
by hazard	durch Zufall 2 Ts/3
head of department	*Abteilungsleiter/in LP 3*
heating	Heizung 4 Ts/4
hiccup	Schluckauf haben 5/3
hiss	zischen 5/3
hit*	schlagen, treffen 3/4
honesty	Ehrlichkeit 12/1
household goods	Haushaltsartikel 13/2
humiliated	*gedemütigt LP 3*

I

immortality	Unsterblichkeit LP 4
in the end	schließlich 12/2
inadequacy	Unzulänglichkeit 1/1
inappropriate	unangebracht, unange-messen LP 3
indefinite article	unbestimmter Artikel 2/4
input* data	Daten eingeben 1/2
insert	einwerfen 13/1

interactive technology	interaktive Technologie 16/1
intimidating	einschüchternd LP 3
inverted commas	Anführungsstriche 3 Ts/6
itch	Jucken; jucken 12/2

J

jumbled	durcheinandergewürfelt 1/4
jump	springen 2 Ts/3

K

in keeping with	in/im Einklang mit 16 Ts/4
knock	(an)klopfen 3/5

L

label	benennen 2/4
Labour Bureau	Arbeitsamt 4/2
law	Rechtswesen, Gesetz 11/1
leak	*Leck LP 4*
lettering for posters	Buchstaben auf Plakate malen, Schrift für Plakate zeichnen 3/1
liar	Lügner/in 9/1
lie*	lügen 6/1
lighter fuel	Feuerzeugbenzin 7/3
lively	lebhaft 16/7
living wage	ausreichender Lohn 4/2
local council school	örtliche öffentliche Schule, „Volksschule" 3/1
Look after yourself!	Paß auf dich auf! 16/6
lose*	verlieren 3/4

M

maintain	halten 12/1
make* sick	*zum Erbrechen bringen LP 1*
margin	Seitenrand 13/5
mend	wiederherstellen, reparieren 6/1
mew	miauen 5/3
microwave	Mikrowelle 2/2
in the midst of	mitten in 9/2
mishear*	sich verhören 12/5
missus	„bessere Hälfte", (Ehe-) Frau 5/2
moo	muhen 5/3
moody	launisch 7/3
mourn someone	*um jdn trauern LP 4*

N

nasty	*schlimm, scheußlich LP 1*
naughty	*böse, gemein LP 1*
neigh	wiehern 5/3
network	Netzwerk 2 Ts/3
newsdesk	Nachrichtenredaktion 14 Ts/3
noun	Substantiv, Hauptwort 2/4

nuclear family	Kleinfamilie, Kernfamilie 5/2
nurse	Krankenschwester 1/2
district <u>nurse</u>	Gemeindeschwester 3/1
nursery for children	Kindertagesstätte, Kindergarten 11/1

O

object	Zweck, Ziel 13/4
object	Einwände haben 13/4
oblige	zwingen 4/2
obsessed with	*besessen von LP 4*
obtain	erhalten 4/2
occasion	Gelegenheit 2 Ts/3
occur	zustande kommen 9/2
odd	seltsam, komisch 6/1
offend	beleidigen, Anstoß erregen 12/2
Oh Lord!	*Ach du lieber Gott! LP 3*
old folks	„alte Leutchen", die Alten 5/2
miss an <u>opportunity</u>	eine Gelegenheit verpassen 2/1
orange-flavoured	*mit Orangengeschmack LP 1*
ordinary conversations	Alltagsgespräche, normale Gespräche 9/4
out of place	nicht angebracht 5/2
outrageous	*unverschämt LP 3*
overall understanding	Grobverstehen 14/3
overwhelmingly	mit überwältigender Mehr- heit, überwältigend 11/1

P

panel of experts	*Expertenrunde LP 2*
pant	keuchen 5/3
paragraph	Absatz, Abschnitt 3/1
participate	teilnehmen 16/7
particularly	besonders, insbesondere 1/1
passage	Abschnitt 3/7
peak	*Höhepunkt, Glanzzeit LP 4*
pick up	in die Hand nehmen 3/1
pity	schade 6/1
polyandry	Polyandry, Vielmännerei 5/2
polygamy	Polygamy, Vielweiberei 5/2
possessive pronoun	Possessivpronomen, besitz- anzeigendes Fürwort 2/4
poverty	Armut 15/1
pram	Kinderwagen LP 1/2
prat	*Trottel LP 3*
prevention	Vorbeugung 7/3
previous	vorausgegangen 14/2
protective clothing	Schutzkleidung 13/1
public transport	öffentliche Verkehrsmittel 9/5
punch	*boxen LP 2*
purpose	*Absicht LP 1*

on <u>purpose</u>	*extra, absichtlich LP 1*
that's a good way of <u>putting</u> it	*so kann man es nennen LP 3*
put* off	abhalten von 2/1
put* through	verbinden (Telefon) 11/3
puzzle something out	etwas enträtseln 9/2

R

model <u>railway</u>	Modelleisenbahn 3/2
range	Reihe, Auswahl 13/6
reasonably priced	mit vernünftigen Preisen 13 Ts/2a
recreate sentences	Sätze wieder zusammen- setzen 7/4
refer to	*sprechen von, erwähnen LP 3*
referral	*Überweisung LP 2*
reflexive pronoun	Reflexivpronomen, rückbe- zügliches Fürwort 2/4
refuse	verweigern, sich weigern 3/5
regret	*Bedauern LP 4*
reject	ablehnen 2/2
reject	Ausschußware 13/4
rejuvenate	verjüngen LP 4
remote	entlegen, abgelegen 1/1
report	Zeugnis 16/7
request	um etw. bitten, etw. verlangen, nach etw. fragen 3/5
request	*Bitte LP 3*
restore	reparieren, wiederher- stellen 14/1
revive	wieder zum Leben erwecken LP 4
ridiculous	lächerlich 10/4
ring*	anrufen, läuten 3/4
rise*	aufstehen, ansteigen 3/4
rule	Regel 2 Ts/3
run* a shop	ein Geschäft führen 1/2

S

sacrifice	opfern 8/5
special <u>sale</u>	Sonderangebot 13 Ts/2a
sample	anschauen, probelesen 15/3
save	aufheben, aufbewahren 1/5
scarce	selten 5/2
scholarship	Stipendium 3/1
screen	Bildschirm 9/6
security officer	Sicherheitsbeamter, Sicherheitsbeamtin 7/3
seek	suchen 4/2
select	auswählen 10/3
semi-colon	Strichpunkt 3 Ts/6
senior manager	leitende/r Angestellte/r 11/1
sentence	Strafe, Satz 8/5
shit	Scheiße 6/1

shooting club	Schützenverein 11/1
show* promise	zu den besten Hoffnungen berechtigen 16/7
shut*	schließen, zumachen 3/4
shut* up	den Mund halten, die Klappe halten 4 Ts/4
sideways	seitwärts, zur Seite 13/3
sigh	seufzen 5/3
single	Einzelzimmer 11/3
slap someone on the back	*jdm auf den Rücken schlagen LP 3*
sleet	Schneeregen 14/4
slot	Schlitz 13/1
smallpox	Pocken 15/2
snore	schnarchen 5/3
soaking	völlig durchnäßt 14/6
solvent abuse	Schnüffeln (von Klebstoffen etc.) 7/3
Some management style!	*Schöner Führungsstil! LP 3*
her throat was <u>sore</u>	sie hatte Halsschmerzen 5/3
space industry	Raumfahrtindustrie 11/1
leave* <u>space</u> for	Platz lassen für 5/6
spokeswoman	Sprecherin 10/2
sports equipment	Sportartikel 8/7
stab	stechen LP 2
hotel <u>staff</u>	Hotelangestellte (Plural) 11/3
staffing costs	*Personalkosten LP 3*
stake in society	Platz in der Gesellschaft, Anteil an der Gesellschaft 4/2
stand up to someone*	*jdm die Stirn bieten LP 3*
stay	bleiben 6/1
steadily	regelmäßig 16/7
have something <u>stitched</u>*	*etwas nähen lassen LP 2*
strangle	erwürgen LP 1/2
subtitle	Untertitel 9/6
succeed	Erfolg haben, etw. erreichen 4/1
suck up	aufsaugen 2/2
suffix	Suffix, Wortanhängsel 6/3
suffocate	ersticken LP1/2
supper	Abendbrot, Abendessen 3/2
electrical <u>supplies</u>	Stromleitungen, elektrische Versorgung 14/1
surgery	Sprechzimmer, Praxis 1/2
swine	Schwein (als Schimpfwort) 6/1
switch	Schalter 11/3
switchboard	Telefonzentrale 11/3

T

Take* care now.	Mach's gut. 16/6
take* it from me	das kannst du mir glauben 8/5

fail to <u>take one's turn</u>	nicht das Wort ergreifen, den Gesprächsfaden nicht aufgreifen 9/2
take* responsibility	Verantwortung übernehmen 10/1
take* up meditation	lernen, zu meditieren 5/1
tax	besteuern 13/4
technical instruction	Gebrauchsanweisung für technische Geräte 13/6
temporary contract	*Zeitvertrag LP 3*
tend to	dazu neigen 16 Ts/4
tension	Anspannung 5/1
the previous one	das Vorangegangene 2/5
threat	Bedrohung 12/1
thumb	Daumen 6/4
tiny	klein, winzig 9/2
tip	kippen, umkippen, Trinkgeld geben 3/5
topic area	Themengebiet 2/5
trial	Gerichtsverfahren, Prozeß 4/2
trigger	*auslösen LP 2*
truth	Wahrheit 6/1
turn	umblättern 12/6
typeset	setzen (Verlagswesen) 14 Ts/3
typhoid	Typhus 15/1

U

unconscious	bewußtlos LP 1/2
upset* nature's balance	das Gleichgewicht der Natur stören 10/3

V

vacancies	freie Zimmer 11/3
vacuum cleaner	Staubsauger 2/2
valuable	wertvoll 5/5
value	wertschätzen 10/3
vet	Tierarzt, Tierärztin 11/1
village elders	Dorfälteste 1/1
violent	gewalttätig LP 2
vital	lebenswichtig 5/2
vote	Wahlrecht 15/2
vulnerable	*angreifbar, verwundbar LP 3*

W

way over length	viel zu lang 14 Ts/3
it's the thin end of the <u>wedge</u>	„so fängt's immer an", (es ist das scharfe Ende des Keils) 10/2
What on earth!	Was um alles in der Welt! 8/4
Wicked!	*Toll! Klasse! LP 4*
widowed	verwitwet 4/2
windscreen wipers	Scheibenwischer 13/1
wonder	sich fragen 3/5